Indicates where a major body type has been directly derived from a previous body type

Indicates a major body type change

1950s	1960s	1970s	1980s	1990s

Special Convertibles

1953
orado Convertible (first)

1960
Eldorado Biarritz Convertible

1973
Eldorado Convertible

1985
Eldorado Biarritz Convertible

1992
Allante North Star Convertible

ndard Convertibles

1957
'62' Convertible

1964
de Ville Convertible

Hardtop Coupes

1953
'62' Coupe de Ville

1960
'62' Coupe

1970
Coupe de Ville

Coupes

1980
Coupe de Ville Cabriolet

1991
Coupe de Ville

Special Coupes

1967
Eldorado Coupe (first)

1978
Eldorado Biarritz Coupe

1980
Eldorado Biarritz

1992
Eldorado

Hardtop Sedans

1956
'62' Sedan de Ville

1963
Sedan de Ville

1972
Sedan de Ville

Sedans

1982
de Ville Sedan

1990
Sedan de Ville

Sedans

1950
'62' Sedan

1968
Fleetwood '60 Special' Brougham Sedan

1971
Fleetwood '60 Special' Brougham

1980
Fleetwood Brougham

1992
Brougham Sedan

Special Sedan

1957
Eldorado Brougham

Special Sedans

1975
Seville

1980
Seville Elegante

1992
Seville

1982
Cimarron

mousines

1959
'75' Limousine

1969
Fleetwood Limousine

1973
Limousine

1982
Fleetwood Limousine

1990
Presidential Limousine

GREENBERG'S®
GUIDE TO
CADILLAC
MODELS AND TOYS

GREENBERG'S® GUIDE TO CADILLAC MODELS AND TOYS

JEFFREY C. GURSKI

Original drawings by Robert Straub

GREENBERG PUBLISHING COMPANY, INC.

Greenberg Publishing Company, Inc.
7566 Main Street
Sykesville, Maryland 21784
(410) 795-7447

First Edition

Manufactured in the United States of America

Greenberg Publishing Company, Inc. publishes the world's largest selection of American and European toy train publications as well as books on Marx, Aurora, Buddy L, pressed steel and firefighting toys. For a complete listing of current Greenberg publications, please call 1-800-533-6644 or write to Kalmbach Publishing Company, 21027 Crossroads Circle, Waukesha, Wisconsin 53187.

Greenberg Shows, Inc. sponsors *Greenberg's Great Train, Dollhouse and Toy Shows*, the world's largest of its kind. The shows feature operating train layouts, dollhouses, and collectible toys. Shows are scheduled along the East Coast each year from Massachusetts to Florida. For a list of our current shows please call (410) 795-7447 or write to Greenberg Shows, Inc., 7566 Main Street, Sykesville, Maryland 21784 and request a show brochure.

Greenberg Auctions, a division of Greenberg Shows, Inc., offers nationally advertised auctions of toy trains and toys. Please contact our auction manager at (410) 795-7447 for further information.

ISBN 0-89778-288-7

Library of Congress Cataloging-in-Publication Data

Gurski, Jeffrey C., 1949–
Greenberg's guide to Cadillac models and toys / Jeffrey C. Gurski
: original drawings by Robert Straub.
p. cm.
Includes index.
ISBN 0-89778-288-7 : $49.95
1. Cadillac automobile—Models—Collectors and collecting.
I. Greenberg Publishing Company. II. Title. III. Title: Guide to Cadillac models and toys.
TL237.G87 1992
629.22'122—dc20 92–6817
CIP

CONTENTS

ACKNOWLEDGMENTS

Thanks to my wife **Nola Gurski** and my mother **Harriet Gurski** for their patience and support during research, draftings, and revision of this effort. I could not have started — much less finished — such a project without their help.

I owe a special debt to my friend **Roger Bartelt** for planting the seed for this project and for providing wise advice and the use of his extensive library.

I appreciate the patience and good humor of a brace of readers who previewed stages of the manuscript and set me straight on errors and misconceptions. Thanks again to **Roger Bartelt**, and to **Robert Bruce**, **Dale Dannefer**, **Michael Dency**, **William Graver**, **Sam Miller**, **Warren Miller**, and **Ferdinand Zegel**.

Many thanks to my longtime friend **Bob Straub** for his original illustrations for the Cadillac family tree of body styles. Bob graciously took time out from his busy schedule doing industrial design work to recall his days as a GM automotive designer and add his expertise to this celebration of the Cadillac motorcar. I have long admired Bob's work and valued his friendship, and I am proud to finally have had the opportunity to work with him on a common project.

Famed collector and friend Ferd Zegel unselfishly loaned me better than two dozen prized models from his outstanding collection to help make the photo shoot more complete. His knowledge and generosity are greatly appreciated by all.

Thanks go to **David Glass**, friend, auto historian, and noted auto emblem and mascot collector, for the loan of the beautiful cloisonné Cadillac radiator emblem pictured herein and for his willingness to share his great knowledge of classic Cadillac motorcars.

Finally, the networking and support of the members of **The Capital Miniature Auto Collectors' Club** helped me locate models, catalog information, and find peace of mind all during the three years of compiling the information for this book. In this connection, thanks to: **Roger Bartelt**, **Harold Blevins**, **Jim Brostrom**, **Douglas Campbell**, **Bud Capron**, **Perry Eichor**, **Andy German**, **Ron Gladish**, **Joe Golabiewski**, **Bill Graver**, **Phil Graves**, **Art Henriques**, **Roger Hirschland**, **Jud Holcombe**, **Vaughn Holcombe**, **Gary Kave**, **Bud Lewis**, **Bob Marshall**, **Fred Maxwell**, **Warren Miller**, **Bill Patton**, **Jim Warrington**, **Stu Wesley**, **Bud Wilkinson**, **Ferd Zegel**, and the club's indefatigable leader and booster — **Charles Francis Wilding**.

My thanks too to several staff members at Greenberg Publishing Company who helped prepare this book for publication. **Elsa van Bergen** edited the final versions of the text and listings and developed the book's format. **Richard M. Watson** edited the index of miniatures. **Brad Schwab** and **Alan Fiterman** photographed all the models, **Brian Falkner** planned the design of this book and its cover, and **Wendy Burgio** did the layout and paste-up. **Donna Price** proofread the manuscript for accuracy and consistency. **Samuel Baum** provided overall support for the project.

Jeffrey C. Gurski
1992

For Chet Gurski — the Cadillac of Dads

INTRODUCTION

While great marques such as Pierce Arrow, Packard, and Duesenberg have long since become only memories of what once was, Cadillac has continued to produce fine American automobiles for better than three-quarters of a century. Cadillacs reflect a vision of what discerning motorists want in luxury transportation. This American automotive dream has been chronicled surprisingly well by Cadillac models and toys. The purpose of this book is to provide insight into the long history of Cadillac models and toys as well as of the motorcar that inspired these miniatures.

Cadillac, from its earliest days, was known for setting the pace in styling and innovation. Automotive genius Henry Leland founded the company that went on to introduce this 1915 V-8 ***(left)****...a new streamlined look in the 1930s* ***(below)****, exemplified by this 1937 coupe...and the standards of elegance and performance appreciated by full-sized and miniature car owners throughout the world (New York Public Library Picture Collection).*

HOW THIS BOOK IS ORGANIZED

The organizing framework of the book is the evolution of the Cadillac automobile, 1903 to the present. Arranged chronologically (according to the date of the Cadillac itself), each section consists of three parts. The first chronicles the development of the Cadillac automobile during a certain time span, usually a year. The second part surveys all known miniatures that have been made of the cars of that period (not all years of Cadillac production have been documented by models or toys). For example, if a manufacturer produced in 1990 a model of a 1937 Cadillac, that model would be discussed under 1937. Finally, the third part summarizes information about all miniatures for that period by listing them alphabetically by manufacturer under each time period and providing concise specifications of each miniature and known variations.

In the listings, important details are included in the following order:

- manufacturer and country of manufacture
- serial number (if known; not all models and toys actually have serial numbers)
- the body type of the model or item
- scale — the proportion of the miniature to the full-size car — or size (if scale is not known or believed not to be accurate, a bumper-to-bumper measurement of the model in inches is given; some items were never made to be scale models)
- material and type of construction
- color — *if* it is believed to have been manufactured in only one color, or if a specific color is significant to a collector. For example, if a variation has some importance, such as being produced for a gift set, that will be cited; if a model or toy has been produced in a number of colors, we will not mention that fact.
- whether the model is current (still being produced) or obsolete (no longer in production)
- a relative rarity rating (how hard it will be to find a specific model)
- additional notes, as relevant
- a range of suggested values or prices, from a low for damaged or playworn examples to a high value for excellent to mint-boxed pieces.

While the author, consulting readers, and editors made every effort to track down accurate information about all known models and toys, there is always the possibility that a Cadillac miniature has eluded our search. Any reader having knowledge of other miniatures or variations not listed is invited to pass this along to Jeff Gurski, c/o Greenberg Publishing Company, 7566 Main Street, Sykesville, Maryland 21784.

At the back of the book there is an index of Cadillac models and Cadillac-inspired toys organized by manufacturer, which provides another way, in addition to the chronological listings and the photographs and captions, of locating a description of a specific model. Within each manufacturer's inventory, models and toys are listed by the years of Cadillacs replicated.

TERMS, RATINGS, AND VALUES IN THIS BOOK

Some of the terms and classifications mentioned above need explanation. While experienced collectors will be familiar with much of what follows, there are also some terms and classifications with special application in this book.

Body Type

In the spirit of "one picture is worth a thousand words," study the illustration on the endpapers, which diagrams the evolution of the Cadillac profile from its roots in horse-and-buggy days. In tracing the Cadillac family tree, it was of course not possible to illustrate every model. Styles from representative years were selected. Note the vertical bars, which indicate a break in the line. It is important to understand that eventually various Cadillac models sported names that did not always reflect the origins of their labels. Brougham, for example, became a model name, along with Eldorado or Sedan de Ville, but this does not mean Brougham necessarily was a derivation of the early closed carriage with outside driver's compartment.

Model Type

The basic types of models are described below.

Factory-made or handbuilt models for collectors

These are the finished models, usually painted, which can be purchased at toy stores, through collectors' subscription services, etc. "Factory-built" is often used interchangeably with "built-up." Some small companies give a choice of less expensive, unassembled kit versions (see *boxed kits* below) of the same model, to allow collectors to save the costs of the labor of final assembly and painting.

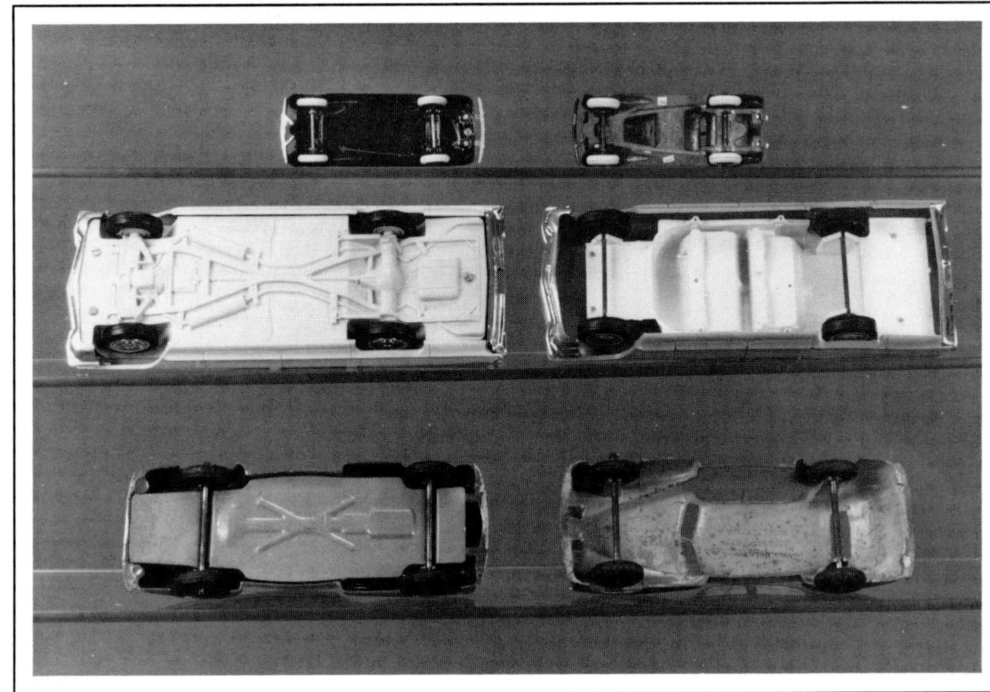

Examining the undersides of models is an important part of building a collection. How the chassis and baseplate are constructed tells a lot about quality, whether a model is a reissue or not, etc. Shown here are chassis details of ***(top)*** *1934 La Salles Buccaneer cast "white" metal,* ***left,*** *and the Tootsietoy die-cast which it reproduces,* ***right; (middle)*** *1961 60 Specials, Jo-Han plastic kit and Korris Kars vinyl, where the body is assumed to be a copy of the Jo-Han model;* ***(bottom)*** *1941 Series 62 sedan, die-cast by Hubley (deluxe version came with steel plate chassis).*

Gift sets

Often, manufacturers sell groupings of models in special packaging. The most desirable gift sets include models with unique colors, markings, or features not included with regular issues. Boxed gift sets are prized collector pieces with greater potential for appreciation. Even distinctive models from broken sets usually command higher collector prices than their regular issue counterparts by virtue of lower production.

Promotional models

Designed to attract interest in GM's current automobile models, these accurate models have been distributed through dealerships and often produced in the actual colors available for that year.

Boxed kits

Modelers purchase kits, of varying complexity, and assemble scale model cars, sometimes painting them and adding touches to customize their models. Kits may contain model parts and accessories made of plastic, metal, fiberglass, or even plaster.

Factory-assembled kits or *factory-made counter samples*

This refers to a sample of a model assembled at the factory for display purposes. Often manufacturers would give retailers already-assembled samples of their model kits to display to prospective buyers who lacked imagination; they could see instantly what the completed model would look like. Factory-made samples are coveted by collectors and command high prices.

It is important for collectors to realize that for some models there might be the originally issued model or kit and then one or more reissues; a collector needs to learn the ways to identify which is which. Additionally there are reproductions and copies, often by companies other than the original manufacturer.

Other types and modifications

Variations is a general term to describe different versions of a basic model (i.e., new colors, alternate body styles, special markings, etc.) Gift sets, commemorative editions, and manufacturers' attempts to spark new interest in older offerings by simple modifications give collectors such variations on a theme to add to their collections.

Some models are called "conversions." Collectors and enterprising cottage-industry modelmakers often save themselves the high costs of starting from scratch to make expensive model tooling by using a standard production model and then modifying it to create a new variation that might otherwise be unavailable. Such models are referred to as "conversions" or "chops." This is a very popular practice in Europe.

Aftermarket items allow a collector and/or model builder to customize a miniature. Just as owners of real cars go to stores like Western Auto or Pep Boys for auto accessories and parts not available from the factory, model collectors and builders often turn to cottage-industry manufacturers for special customizing parts such as

Cadillac models and toys come in a variety of materials, and some miniatures have special functions. ***Top:*** *Structo's die-cast 1950 coupe from car-carrier set and a 1980 Seville coin bank, slush-cast and plated pot metal, by unknown manufacturer (the coin slot is in the rear window).* ***Middle:*** *1938 Series 75 town car as Avon's after-shave lotion bottle and a pressed sand-and-glue 1959 convertible, mislabeled Eldorado, from Mr. Sandman's 1950's Dream Machines.* ***Bottom:*** *Hubley's 1941 Series 62 die-cast sedan and sedan taxi.*

decals, new castings, etc. to complete conversion from a standard model or kit offering to a special version not otherwise available.

Materials and Construction Processes

The materials and processes used to manufacture the Cadillac models and toys described in this book fall into six basic categories.

Tinplate (or more correctly, pressed steel)

The French and Germans pioneered the method of pressing thin lithographed sheets of steel into shaped toy parts. These parts were assembled to make colorfully elaborate toys, some of which were powered by clockwork motors. Examples of such early toys are prized collectibles today. However, it was the Japanese who built an entire toy industry out of the ruins of World War II by recycling thin sheet metal — often from old cans (hence, the nickname "tin") — into imaginative and wonderfully inexpensive toys. Tinplate toys have all but died off for a number of reasons. Some poorly made toys had dangerous sharp edges. Some paints used contained lead. The better toys were prohibitively labor-intensive in a market where labor was becoming increasingly expensive. Finally, plastics technology of the 1950s and 1960s revolutionized the economics of toymaking. Japanese tinplate cars are very expensive and desirable today because they were the throwaways of yesterday and often unappreciated in their own day. As a result, survivors are few, and their relative rarity drives prices upward as collectors rediscover the charm and color of the tin toy.

Slush-molded pot metal

This method of casting was cheap and fast. Molten pot metal (a hard and brittle alloy) was slushed about to coat the inside of a hollow mold. The excess molten metal was drained from the slush mold, and a hollow casting was the result. Vehicles that were slush molded were durable but lean on fine detail. Many small companies produced such toys well into the 1960s.

Die-cast

Die-casts are metal models from costly steel dies prepared by skilled pattern makers working from a wooden master model. A typical die-cast model may require many separate metal castings, as well as additional plastic and rubber castings for windows, tires, interior, and bumpers. Die-cast models are produced by toy companies that can afford the high costs of preparing such complex tools, mounting elaborate promotions, warehousing, and maintaining distribution systems. Die-casts are made in large numbers to spread out these costs. The Dowst brothers of Chicago pioneered and perfected this process in the 1920s and went on to found the Tootsietoy empire.

Die-cast models are made from molten zinc alloy injected under great pressure into the steel dies. Since the tools for die-casting are of the hardest steel and precision-made, models can be produced at high speed

Some collectors search for models and toys of a certain material. Although rubber toys appear to be crude miniatures next to many die-casts, they are increasingly rare and valuable. Pictured here ***(top)****, Arcor's 1950 Series 62 sedan and* ***(below)*** *Auburn's 1946 styling dream car.*

and over a long production run. After castings are cleaned and polished, they are painted and assembled on assembly lines. Mass production and fierce competition usually make die-cast models relative bargains for collectors. A company with unpopular offerings seldom lasts long.

Plastic

Plastic models and kits first appeared in quantity after World War II. Even though cast in high-pressure molds — as die-cast metals are — plastics are easier to finish and less expensive to make than metal. Plastics can be molded in colors or flash-plated to simulate polished chrome. Acetate plastic was used in promotional automotive models from the early 1950s until the early 1960s when it was replaced by nonwarping cycolac and polystyrene. Fine detail and ease of construction in polystyrene model kits virtually destroyed the market for comparatively crude wooden model kits in the 1950s. As a result, plastic dominates the mass-produced model kit market to this day.

Resin

Fiberglass-resin or epoxy-resin models are cast from soft silicone or rubber molds that wear quickly and thus limit production to short runs. Because the cost cannot be amortized over thousands of models, resin models are pricey. Often such models are the work of dedicated car modelers who produce kits or finished models as alternatives to those mass-produced by the big modelmaking companies. Many exceptional resin models have fine details such as nameplates and trim done in photo-etched metal and/or high-quality decals. Resin kits are generally more trouble to build than the more commonly available injection-molded plastic kits because they require more finishing, and they vary widely in quality.

Experiments, folk art, and handmade one-offs

While mass-producers of toys may seem to limit themselves to metal and plastic, creative modeler builders have proven a more adventurous lot. Scratch-built models and very low-production pieces have been made from soft "white" metals, wood, plaster, paper/cardboard, or even scrap materials. *"White" metal* is a generic term to describe a family of inexpensive alloys that melt at relatively low temperatures and lend themselves to capturing fine detail in molds. Such castings are popular with hobbyists because they generally are soft enough to be cleaned and polished with a hobby knife, files, and sandpaper.

Sometimes noncommercial models are crude, but skilled builders have also created charming one-off (one-of-a-kind or preproduction) masterpieces. Just because a model is not made in huge quantities does not mean it is not desirable. There is an undeniable exclusivity in owning such a model.

See the glossary at the end of this Introduction for further explanation of terms used in the construction of models and toys, as well as of automobiles.

Relative Rarity Ratings

There are in this book five general categories that indicate how difficult it might be to obtain a specific model.

Common (but desirable)

These pieces are usually current issues and readily available at stores. The best time to buy!

Less common

Models and toys with this rating are still available with a little searching but are not considered rare. Many "less common" pieces have only recently gone out of production and general distribution. Still others are available only through specialized dealers and may require some detective work and/or mail order.

Rare

These pieces have usually been out of production and distribution for some time. These items have become rare and are available mainly at antique and specialty shows and through networks of collectors. Asking prices may vary widely at this stage.

Very rare

Models and toys with this rating are very rare, desirable, and difficult to find. These are often sought by serious collectors, and hobby networking usually limits buying, selling, and trading to a closed circle. Casual collectors get very uncomfortable with prices accompanying "very rare" pieces.

Rarest

This rating is reserved for the rarest and most desirable collectibles. Collectors' prices reflect this distinction, and values continue to spiral upward to stratospheric heights. Not for the fainthearted!

Note that the ratings listed in this book indicate *relative* rarity; some collectors might feel the term "rare" should describe only those models that are extremely hard to find, but here that term designates a model that is harder to find than the comparatively common ones but not as difficult to find as still other models. Note also that relative rarity takes into account availability and desirability among collectors. The most expensive models or toys are not necessarily the rarest. Finally, note that in addition to a phrase to indicate relative rarity the listings in this book also contain notations to indicate whether a piece is current or obsolete. The suggested price guidelines at the end of each listing reflect the condition of a piece within the general relative rarity rating.

Range of Suggested Values

Collectors and dealers should realize that values fluctuate with condition, regional demand, and changes in collectors' tastes; any values given in this book are *suggestions.* In bold type at the end of each listing you will find a range of suggested prices, based on observations of selling prices of pieces ranging from "damaged or playworn" to "mint or excellent."

Suggested values for damaged or playworn pieces reflect market demand for salvageable items. Badly damaged items are best sold only as "parts cars" at still further reduction. Scratches, dents, chips, and broken or missing parts proportionally reduce the value of even the rarest and most desirable models and toys.

A mint-boxed promotional model or die-cast is a flawless example of brand new or new old stock (NOS, boxed models that have sat on store shelves for years) — with model *and* box in excellent condition. Deduct 10 to 15 percent for missing factory packaging for an otherwise perfect piece. A mint or excellent kit means unbuilt and in the original box. Values for *built* kits are considerably less.

TIPS FOR BEGINNING COLLECTORS

Collecting miniature Cadillacs is only one specialized focus in the larger hobby of miniature-car collecting. Indeed, few collections are exactly alike because the tastes

Clearly, this group of miniatures has special appeal to racing fans. Closest to the Shell station, each with "3" on the side, are 1950 Cunningham Le Mans coupes: AMR kit model to left, Vitesse model in front of gas station, Manou's handcarved wood model to rear; to left foreground is Le Monstre racing car kit from John Day (#2); and to far right is the glossy green Cadillac-powered Allard J2X roadster, from Grand Prix Models kit.

and likes and dislikes of the collector are reflected in the items that are coveted and rejected in the course of building a collection. There are several ways to approach collection-building, and a collector may choose to limit the focus of his or her collection or to expand it to suit individual tastes. Some suggestions for organizing a collection follow.

Organizing a Collection

By scale

Some enthusiasts prefer the 1/25 scale commonly used in promotional models or in kits. Manufacturers such as Revell, AMT, MPC, Monogram, and others generally standardize the scales of their offerings to encourage repeat customers for their wares. Still other collectors prefer 1/48- or 1/43-scale model automobiles because they are the proper size for Lionel and/or American Flyer train layouts. Collectors often also have their own reasons for rejecting a particular size of model or toy, such as limited display or storage space.

By manufacturer

Many collectors seek out examples of each item a certain manufacturer produces. This kind of collecting allows the use of a manufacturer's catalog to organize a collection. Note that the index of all Cadillac-inspired models and toys by manufacturer, which appears at the back of this book, will be helpful to collectors who favor particular brands of miniatures: it provides another way of locating descriptions of specific models and a checklist for collections organized around one or more manufacturers.

By style or material

Some collectors seek out only metal models while others seek only plastic. The die-hard Banthrico metal bank collector, for example, might not want to have anything to do with a plastic promotional car of the same vintage or vice versa.

By make

This book has grown out of seeking models of any scale or material on the theme of miniature Cadillacs. Part of the adventure is in tracing the history of the real car and finding different interpretations of the car through the miniatures.

By price level

Some collectors limit themselves to items below a certain predetermined price. The question of exceeding a collecting budget thus never becomes a problem.

By current or obsolete issue

Some collectors limit themselves to only obsolete models while others limit themselves to only the most current.

By fidelity to detail

Some collectors favor only those models that are true to detail. Cartoonish toys or ceramic car candy dishes would have no place in such collections.

By appeal

All of the ways of building a collection suggested above are arbitary, and collectors are the best judges of what they like best. Indeed, impressive collections have been built out of individual responses to specific models — out of buying a model simply because the collector likes it for some aesthetic or personal reason (such as wanting a model of the old family car). Often a collector's taste or purpose might change before a collection is complete, and a whole new direction might emerge.

Making Major Purchases

A beginning collector faces the frustration of wanting to build a collection quickly. This is fine if money is not a consideration, but even the wealthy like to get best value. Tips to help you get the most from your collector dollar follow.

1. Buy quality. At first it is tempting to snatch up every item that comes along, but remember that in the long run it is wiser to buy one fine piece for your collection than a dozen battered, scratched, or broken pieces. This quality vs. quantity rule is hardest for new collectors to remember.
2. Buy mint-boxed examples whenever practical. The finest collectibles with the highest potential for appreciation are the excellent-to-mint-boxed examples. Original packaging can add 10 or 15 percent to the value of an item. This will be a big advantage should you choose to resell the item later. Don't buy restored toys unless you really like them, for their potential for appreciation and a higher resale value is limited.
3. Find out all you can about the collectibles you want to buy. Join a club, read guidebooks, and subscribe to collector journals and hobby magazines. Even if you do not intend to buy by mail order, subscribe to collector tradesheets such as *Trader's Horn*. These publications will identify dealers as new sources and allow you a chance to gauge prices before you put down hard cash.

It is often difficult to obtain manufacturers' catalogs. Sometimes you can get them through dealers — especially if the manufacturer is based in the United States;

other sources include other collectors and dealers at shows. Even if not the most recent issue, a catalog is an extremely useful tool in building and checking your collection. Be warned that toy manufacturers, like many other industries, can change hands frequently and suddenly: because addresses are quickly out of date, we have not included them in our index of models and toys by manufacturer.

4. Look for unusual sources of models. Garage sales, estate sales, antique shops, and even the local classifieds can start you on your way, although as miniature collecting grows, such sources are less fertile ground than they once were. Ask relatives and neighbors to check their attics and basements for old toys and automobilia. Many people are happy to give away treasures that are cluttering up their homes. Better yet, once you have made your wants known to them, your friends and family might watch out for items that could be of interest to you. A little networking usually pays.

5. Attend collectibles shows. Model automobiles frequently show up with regularity at doll or train shows, as well as those focusing on miniature cars. The huge annual auto flea markets like those held at Carlisle and Hershey, Pennsylvania, are loaded with models and toys sprinkled in with the full-sized automobiles. Be sure to get on mailing lists, for there are events virtually every month of the year.

At these shows make it a practice to examine trends in pricing. Different parts of the country have different prices. The Midwest is a hotbed of plastic promotional and model-kit collecting, while the West is more heavily into die-cast models, and there are pockets of specialty collectors from coast to coast.

6. Watch for fakes. It is the real world out there, even in collecting, and a minority of dealers are crooked. Worse yet, some reputable dealers have bought counterfeits from the unscrupulous and then unknowingly resold them to their customers as genuine articles. Do your homework. Take a knowledgeable collector friend along to consult on your major purchases.

7. Watch out for incredibly good deals on large collections. Robbery is not a stranger to toy collecting. Fenced goods are still stolen goods, and if you are caught buying stolen toys and models, you will be out the money you paid and the goods themselves when they are confiscated by the police. Remember, if the deal seems too good to be true, it probably is.

8. A wise rule for all collectors: document your collection. Develop a way to catalog your growing collection, listing items in a data base or a notebook, and photograph important pieces or areas of display shelving. Current manufacturer catalogs will help you prove the worth of your collection, for insurance purposes. Talk to your insurance agent now, not when it's too late.

Further, avoid bragging about rare pieces in your collection to strangers. You might come home one day to find your prized collection gone. Common sense is the best rule for security.

DISPLAYING AND MAINTAINING YOUR COLLECTION

Most collectors are proud of their acquisitions and want to display them so they and others can enjoy looking at them. Small collections are often displayed on mantelpieces, bookshelves, or coffee tables. However, collectors with more than a handful of models soon realize that acquiring a collection is only one part of the collecting process. Two considerations beyond the purchasing stage are finding display space and protecting what can be a considerable investment from damage.

Unless collectors are content with storing boxed models unseen in closets, attics, or garages, the purchase of specialized display cases or shelving is a good idea. Indeed some collectors have set aside entire rooms or *buildings* to display their treasures! Bookcases, display cases, shadow boxes, or special shelving should not only showcase collectibles but protect them as well.

Display areas should be out of the reach of pets and small children. Some models have dangerous sharp edges, parts small enough to swallow, and even poisonous lead paint. Common sense will avert tragedy.

Keep displays out of high-traffic areas in the home. Small models can easily be brushed off a shelf or table and onto the floor to their destruction. In fact, models are probably best left in glassed-in cabinets or displays to avoid damage and dust.

Never leave models in harsh, direct sunlight for long periods of time. The sun will bleach and fade colors, warp plastic, dry out and split rubber tires, and crack and yellow decals very quickly to lower the value of even the finest collectibles. Display cases placed in direct sunlight can become mini-ovens in minutes.

Careless handling can also damage or destroy the value of a model collection. Always support a model from the underside. Handling a model by its fragile parts is asking for trouble and breakage.

Few collectors realize that handling chrome-plated plastic is a bad practice. Skin oils leave acidic deposits that will inexorably eat through the thin plating and etch fingerprints into the surface; these marks cannot be removed short of replating. If plated plastic must be handled, use a clean tissue or a soft cloth.

Dust and dirt can also ruin fine models. While a good quality "dust-proof" display case will help keep your models cleaner longer, all models eventually need cleaning to preserve and maintain their value. Do not *ever* attempt to wipe dust and dirt from a model; it only grinds harmful grit into the pores of the paint, making permanent stains. Instead, wash away accumulated dust, dirt, and fingerprints with a mild solution of dishwashing liquid and warm water. Use a soft sable-hair artist's brush to swirl the solution into tight places, and rinse the soapy model in a bowl of clean cold water. Do not rinse a model under a running faucet, or you may wash tiny irreplaceable parts down the drain! Blot dry with a clean, lint-free, absorbent towel.

Use the mildest detergent available on models and toys. Powerful household cleansers are wonderful for cleaning kitchen countertops and appliances, but they will damage or even strip paint or chrome plating from delicate models.

Tin (pressed-steel) toys should always be kept in dry places. Do not even *think* of washing such treasures in water, for they will rust. Often a patina of dirt and dinginess can be polished away with a clean rag dampened with a good quality liquid automobile cleaner wax. Polish away the haze when the wax dries to reveal a shiny protective coating. Use an old toothbrush to remove dried wax from nooks and crannies.

Clockwork or electric mechanisms can be sprayed with WD-40. The liquid carrier flushes away dust and dirt and then evaporates, leaving a light layer of lubrication and rust preventative behind. Do not use light household oils or motor oils to lubricate, for they attract still more dust and dirt.

GLOSSARY OF STRUCTURAL TERMS FOR CARS AND MINIATURES

baseplate: plate covering the otherwise open underside of a model

body: automotive structure that envelops passengers, engine, and wheels. The body is bolted directly to the chassis on cars with body/frame construction. On more modern "unibody" vehicles, the body becomes a stress-bearing member of the whole assembly (much the same as the fuselage on an airplane) and eliminates the need for a heavy steel chassis framework, thus saving weight.

boot: American automotive term used to describe cloth, canvas, or fiberglass cover for folded convertible top. The British use "boot" to describe what Americans call the "trunk" of a car.

cid (or C.I.D.): abbreviation for cubic-inch displacement, the total volume of space through which the pistons of an engine travel

coachbuilder: independent automotive body designer/contractor. It was common practice for buyers of exclusive automobiles to have the factory ship a running chassis to a custom coachbuilder. The coachbuilder would then custom-design a body to fit the special needs and personality of the new car owner — for a price.

chassis: refers to the frame that support a car's body structure and running gear

continental kit: In the early days of motoring, primitive tire technology often necessitated the carrying of multiple full-sized spare tires because of frequent tire failure. One method of carrying the bulky spare(s) without sacrificing trunk space was to specially mount the spare(s) at the rear of the car over the rear bumper. Designers added elegance to the assembly by shaping elaborate metal tire covers, special bumpers, and farings. Later, when tire reliability improved, the "continental kit" often was retained for its ornamental value. In fact, some were even dummy versions that did not carry a spare tire within their stylized covers!

dream car: See *show car* below.

dual-cowl: two-windshield configuration, whereby rear-seat passengers in an open car also have their own windshield to protect them from the elements. This was a popular and elegant feature of expensive open-tourers and custom-bodied phaetons.

flash-plated: a term used interchangeably with "plated" (by electrochemical means). Many model parts are flash-plated with a thin coat of shiny metal to simulate chrome.

friction drive: A simple inertia flywheel motor is geared to a toy car's wheels. Forward motion spins the flywheel and multiplies the force expended to power the toy car across the playroom floor.

greenhouse: design term for the open glass area of the vehicle's passenger compartment. A larger greenhouse provides better visibility for the driver, a safety concern.

HO scale: refers to 1/87 scale, but model builders and collectors often fudge the term "HO" to refer to small-scale items such as Matchbox-sized cars. This often causes confusion and consternation.

Hot Wheels: registered trademark for Mattel's line of die-cast toy vehicles that pioneered fast-rolling wheeels on nylon bearings on wire axles.

interior tub: Modelmakers often mold the interiors of model cars in one open-topped boxlike assembly that is reminiscent of a "tub" shape. This tub is then fitted to the model during assembly to give the illusion of an interior furnished with floor, seats, instrument panel, and steering wheel.

lake(s) pipes: the car customizers' accessory first popularized by hotrodders who would reroute exhaust through open pipes running along the rocker panels of their racers to exit ahead of the rear wheels. The name probably originated with the specially modified cars that competed for speed records on the dry lakes of California where hotrodding was born.

Laser (lazer) disks: registered trademark for Matchbox's special line of miniature die-cast vehicles decorated with iridescent wheel covers that remind one of tiny compact disks converted to hubcap duty

lithographed: a term taken from lithography, a printing or painting process employed in toymaking, where colors and details are first stamped or rolled onto a flat sheet of thin steel. The plates are then placed in large dies where they are stretched over a form under great pressure. The resulting toy is colorful and three-dimensional.

mag wheel: automotive slang term taken from "magnesium wheel"; it originally indicated a lightweight cast-magnesium rim used on racing cars to save weight. Such wheels were usually open (without hubcaps) and/or slotted to circulate cooling air for brakes. Over the years, manufacturers often imitated the rugged style of these competition wheels and styled look-alike "mags" to give their cars a sporty look. The term has come to mean almost any styled wheel without hubcaps.

Micromachines: registered trademark for tiny pocket-sized toy cars, trucks, boats, and aircraft manufactured by Galoob of China. These popular, brightly colored, cartoonish interpretations of real vehicles are copied by many different toy companies. "Micromachines" has thus become a kind of identification among collectors for this type of toy.

ohv (or O.H.V.): abbreviation for "overhead valve," describing the configuration of intake and exhaust valves on a reciprocating engine

pantograph: a precision tool used to mechanically transfer exact designs or plans to a different scale

photo-etched trim: a process whereby tiny emblems and model trim are transferred to a thin sheet of metal by photographic masking, and then powerful chemicals remove the excess metal and leave the design. Manufacturers are thus able to duplicate tiny emblems and delicate trim for model cars with great fidelity.

pontoon fender: design term used to describe a sleek compound-curve fender that wrapped over and covered much of the tire. Legend, hearsay, and speculation say that this term might have grown out of admiration for some of the aerodynamically designed seaplane air racers of the 1920s and 1930s, all of which rode on sleek pontoon floats that could slice through the air as well as the water.

show car: Special styling studies are done by auto manufacturers to explore new ideas before committing them to full production. The results, show cars, are displayed at auto shows, in auto publications, and at consumer clinics to gauge public opinion. Thus show cars serve as tools to showcase creativity, spark consumer interest, and create an exciting corporate image. The term "show car" is often used interchangeably with "dream car."

side mount(s): a spare tire mounted in a recess in the front fender between the front tire and the door opening. Like the continental kit, the side mount was born of necessity in the era of failure-prone tires. A side-mounted spare saved trunk space, and it enabled engineers to avoid adding dead weight to the very rear of the vehicle where it could affect handling. One added intangible was the side-mounted spare's elegance. Designers draped side mounts in swoopy sheet metal, chrome, and specially fitted canvas covers. This was a favored option on custom-bodied cars.

silkscreened: printing technique whereby paint or ink is squeegeed through the openings of a design matte to leave a design behind when the matte is removed

skirt(s): sculptured sheet-metal filler for the rear wheel opening that partially covers the rear wheel. Customizers used them to make their cars look lower and longer, and their lesson was not lost on Detroit designers who occasionally resurrect the fender skirt to "formalize" the lines of their automotive stylings.

Speedwheels: registered trademark for Matchbox's line of die-cast toy vehicles equipped with fast-rolling wheels on nylon bearings on wire axles. "Speedwheels" are generally regarded among collectors as Matchbox's response to the success of Mattel's popular "Hot Wheels."

styling study: an experimental auto design, often used interchangeably with "dream car"

A NOBLE START 1903–1942

1903–1910

The Automobile

Seventeenth-century French nobleman/explorer LeSieur Antoine de la Monthe Cadillac never could have dreamed that his name and crest would one day be carried on an *automobile* that would be popularly called "the Standard of the World." Why was Cadillac's name chosen? Simple. It was the intrepid Cadillac, who spent thirty years fur trapping and protecting French interests in the wilds of New France and who named a certain river settlement Ville d'Etroit, or "Village of the Straits"; here would rise the city that became the hub of American automotive industry — Detroit.

Cadillac was founded by automotive genius Henry Leland. Leland's early work machining interchangeable firearm components at the Colt factory was a training ground, and there he established his reputation for craftsmanship. For a short time after leaving Colt, Leland established his own shop to subcontract engines for the famous curved-dash Olds. Fate tapped Leland on the shoulder in 1901, when, in one of his legendary snits, auto pioneer Henry Ford left the Henry Ford Company (reorganized from the failing Detroit Automobile Company), leaving Ford's backers looking for direction. Leland stepped in, and the result of the reorganization of the Henry Ford Company was the Cadillac Automobile Company and the first one-cylinder Model A Cadillac.

This model was followed by a series of improved models that established the Cadillac name as synonymous with reliable quality. These early cars were not luxury cars, but they were state-of-the-art road machines, and a step up in price from the competition. Leland's engineering genius and William Metzger's gung-ho sales abilities combined to assure success.

***Top:** 1903 open Cadillac **(left)** and 1910 limousine **(right)** are represented in Gowland & Gowland/Revell plastic kits; they flank a 1906 Tootsietoy die-cast Model K coupe. **Middle:** Die-cast 1913 roadsters from Matchbox Models of Yesteryear with a Cadillac crest radiator emblem, ca. 1918-1925 (David Glass Collection). **Bottom:** 1926 Caddies from Tootsietoy die-cast 1927 GM Series: touring car, #6-05 (Ferd Zegel Collection); sedan, #6-04; roadster, #6-01; commercial delivery, #6-06; coupe, #6-02 (Ferd Zegel Collection).*

By 1904 the Cadillac Automobile Company formally became the Cadillac Motor Car Company, and Leland became general manager. Within a year, Cadillac was producing more cars than any other car company, for Henry Ford's Tin Lizzie was still only a dream.

In a celebrated 1908 demonstration, three randomly selected Cadillacs were torn down and their parts scrambled into separate piles. Under the careful watch of officials of the British Royal Automobile Club, the three piles of components were reassembled into three cars. All three cars started and ran, proving the interchangeability of Cadillac parts. This was unheard-of precision for the day, and Cadillac was shortly thereafter awarded its first Dewar's Trophy for Excellence.

Cadillac did not rest upon its laurels. Soon the venerable one-lung engines gave way to more powerful L-head fours and the impressively successful Model 30 (named appropriately for its horsepower rating). A variety of standard or custom body styles was available to the discriminating motorist. General Motors wheeler-dealer William C. Durant knew a good car when he saw one, so he bought out Cadillac and hired Leland to continue running the operation. Cadillac soon became the jewel in the GM crown.

1903–1910 in Miniature

Among the notable miniatures of these early Cadillacs are (1) the 1/38-scale Gowland and Gowland plastic kit of the 1903 open single-cylinder model (essentially the same as the Gowland and Gowland 1903 Ford plastic kit with an added back seat!), (2) the die-cast 1/48-scale 1906 Tootsietoy Cadillac coupe, and (3) the 1/38-scale Gowland and Gowland plastic kit of the 1910 Model 30 limousine.

The Tootsietoy 1906 coupe resembles the single-cylinder Model K and was part of a crude but charming gift set of die-cast metal classic toy cars released in the 1960s. It is easy to tell these cars from earlier metal Tootsietoys because of the newer issues' use of yellow plastic wheels. The gift set was cleverly packaged in a cardboard box shaped like a book that opened to reveal the toy cars mounted in die-cut openings. A complete boxed set is difficult to find, although individual pieces surface and are largely unappreciated by die-cast collectors.

The Gowland and Gowland kits interest kit collectors for two reasons. First, the Gowland and Gowland series was the first line of plastic model car kits that was available in any significant quantity. The series was part of a wave of new plastic products that appeared in the early 1950s. Although these kits were not greatly detailed, they were easily assembled and probably provided the first taste of plastic-model building for an entire generation of car buffs. Second, the Gowland and Gowland line stayed in distribution for years when re-released under the Revell name. Remarkably, these kits can be found with some regularity at toy and antique shows. The most desirable finds are the factory-built, painted counter samples given to dealers as sales aids to encourage hobbyists to build the whole line of kits. Boxed and unbuilt kits can frequently still be found for but a few dollars. In addition, four-car gift sets cast from the original molds have been reissued only recently. These are not difficult models to find.

1903

Gowland & Gowland/Revell (USA): open style, 1/38, plastic kit; obsolete; less common. **$5 – 15**

1906

Tootsietoy (USA): Model K coupe, 1/48, die-cast; obsolete; less common. One piece from classic car set of 1960s. **$10 – 20**

1910

Gowland & Gowland/Revell (USA) H-39: Model 30 limousine, 1/38, plastic kit; obsolete; less common. **$5 – 15**

1913

The Automobile

Careful market planning and continued technical innovation enabled Cadillac to weather the economic ups and downs of the teens, and the marque steadily improved its position in the marketplace. In 1913 Cadillac was awarded a second Dewar's Trophy in recognition of its revolutionary electrical starter, ignition, and lighting systems which were developed jointly by Henry Leland and Charlie Kettering of the Dayton Engineering Laboratories (DELCO).

Cadillac had evolved into an industry innovator, setting many new standards. The switch to electric starting and lighting introduced the joys of motoring to many who were intimidated by, or impatient with, hand crank starting and inefficient and dangerous acetylene lights. With these changes, auto manufacturers hoped that many more women would be willing to take the wheel, thus opening new markets.

1913 in Miniature

An early leader in the die-cast toy car field was the British Lesney toy company, founders of "Matchbox." One of many long-lived models in Matchbox's famed "Yesteryear" series was their Y-6 1/48-scale 1913 Cadillac roadster, commemorating one of the last four-cylinder Cadillacs made before the 1915 debut of the V-8 engine. The Matchbox Y-6 Cadillac, available in several color combinations over its production run, was replaced in 1978 by a Rolls Royce fire truck! The Matchbox Cadillac roadster was ruggedly built for youngsters' play, so detail is crudely heavy at best. Such simple construction and a long production run assured that many have survived, keeping collector prices at affordable levels.

1913

Matchbox Yesteryear (GB) Y-6: roadster, 1/48, die-cast; obsolete; less common. **$5 – 15**

1926

The Automobile

Bringing Cadillac into the General Motors fold was a godsend for William Durant when, in 1910, he found himself in serious financial trouble; the rock-solid Cadillac and Buick divisions saved the automaking conglomerate from the financial sharks and barracudas. Durant regained his control of GM by the middle of the decade, but many changes had taken place on the automotive and international scene, and General Motors would never again be totally guided by any single individual's vision. The stakes had become too high.

Cadillac moved into the future by pioneering the first American production V-8 engine by the dawn of the Roaring Twenties. The V-8 was rugged, smooth, and compact. As World War I began, Cadillac was the staff car most often used by the army because of its reliability. World War I also drove a wedge between the Durant/Leland relationship when Henry Leland disagreed with Durant on whether GM should get involved in military aircraft-engine production. Leland and his financial-whiz son left to form the Lincoln Motor Company to build aircraft engines for the war effort in addition to fine cars that ultimately would compete directly with Cadillac.

The V-8 Cadillac line served Durant well for the next few years, but by the early 1920s, DuPont family money had helped ease Durant out the corporate door. In 1923 Alfred Sloan assumed the GM presidency. He left the profitable Buick and Cadillac divisions alone, but he reorganized the other car lines in the hope they would do as well.

By 1924 the Leland-designed Cadillac V-8 was history, and a new 83-horsepower V-8 set new industry standards for smoothness. Known as the V-63, this Cadillac became the car of kings and the chassis of choice for custom bodies and for professional vehicles such as limousines and hearses. In 1925 L. P. Fisher, of Fisher Brothers fame, became president of the Cadillac Motor Car Division. By 1926 Fisher Body and Fleetwood Metal Body Company became in-house GM operations. Cadillacs to this day still bear the Fisher and Fleetwood body names.

1926 in Miniature

The 1926 Tootsietoy GM Series celebrated this monumental year for General Motors. Manufactured by the Chicago-based Dowst Manufacturing Company, this simple toy car series consisted of Buick, Cadillac, Chevrolet, and Oldsmobile chassis to which brougham, coupe, delivery truck, roadster, sedan, and touring-car bodies were attached. Hence, there were twenty-four possible chassis/body combinations. This was a long-lived production series, and in 1933 a no-name chassis with a plain, unmarked radiator joined the line. Tootsietoy/General Motors fans often refer to this no-name issue as an Oakland. Fine details were vague, but with the exception of the Oakland chassis, the car names were emblazoned diagonally on the radiators in huge, out-of-scale lettering.

The Cadillac version apparently came in all body variations. Contrasting chassis/body color combinations using blue, black, gray, green, red, tan, and yellow were common. However, since the bodies were not difficult to interchange, accurate documentation of production variations and color combinations becomes difficult. All cars rode on steel disk wheels on pin-type axles crimped on one end. These tiny cars were durable playthings and, with the exception of the delicate roadster and touring-car windshields, could withstand years of kiddie sandbox torture and still survive. Remarkably, many are still around for collectors to enjoy today.

1926

Tootsietoy (USA) 6-01: roadster, 3", die-cast; obsolete; rare. Part of 1927 GM series. **$35 – 95**

Tootsietoy (USA) 6-02: coupe, 3", die-cast; obsolete; rare. Part of 1927 GM series. **$35 – 95**

Tootsietoy (USA) 6-03: brougham (round quarter-windows, landau irons), 3", die-cast; obsolete; rare. Part of 1927 GM series. **$35 – 95**

Tootsietoy (USA) 6-04: sedan (rectangular quarter-windows), 3", die-cast; obsolete; rare. Part of 1927 GM series. **$35 – 95**

Tootsietoy (USA) 6-05: touring car, 3", die-cast; obsolete; rare. Part of 1927 GM series. **$35 – 95**

Tootsietoy (USA) 6-06: delivery truck, 3", die-cast; obsolete; rare. Part of 1927 GM series. **$35 – 95**

1927–1930

The Automobile

In 1927 Fisher Body hired a talented Californian who would forever change the way Americans looked at their cars. Stylist Harley Earl established General Motors' Art and Color Section, one of the industry's first full-blown auto *styling* studios. It was Earl who was largely responsible for establishing the tradition of the annual model change and for creating the natty new La Salle that filled the void between the most expensive Buick and the lowest-line Cadillac. The La Salle was such a popular new model that it paced the 1927 Indy 500 race, a prestigious duty! Earl also penned designs for a variety of new sleek body styles and chose chic colors that rivaled anything that soberly proper Packard or Lincoln offered. The 1928 models were well received, and sales were good.

Then came the Great Crash of 1929. Lawrence Fisher guided Cadillac through perilous economic times with remarkable skill and despite the precipitous drop in demand for cars, unveiled Cadillac's most magnificent automobile to date, the V-16, in 1930. A year later a V-12 was introduced with much less hoopla. Rivals had nothing even close to compete with these engineering marvels. While these super cars were well received by those who could still afford such luxuries, during the Great Depression they were the wrong products for the hard economic times ahead.

1927–1930 in Miniature

Solido toymakers of France replicated the 452-cubic inch V-16 Fleetwood-bodied landaulette of 1930 with remarkable fidelity in 1⁄43 scale. One could easily visualize some potentate or captain of industry chauffeured about the town in such an elegant land yacht.

1930

Solido (France) 4085: landaulette, 1⁄43, die-cast; current; common. **$6 – 18**

1931–1932

The Automobile

The splendidly refined V-16 Cadillacs were identified by letters to indicate their model years. While there was no letter designation for 1930 models, 1931 models were labeled Series A, 1932 models were B, 1933 models were C, and 1934 and 1935 were D. Brilliant designer Harley Earl dazzled the dwindling luxury car market of Depression-dogged America with an array of striking Cadillac body styles that were the dream cars for an era that crushed dreams.

It is also worthy to note that a V-12-powered Cadillac paced the 1931 Indianapolis 500, only four years after the last Cadillac product was honored with the task. Time would allow the marque to return to the Brickyard again and again in later years.

Fortunately for miniature-Cadillac collectors, many toymakers and model-kit manufacturers made, and still make, replicas of several of these important cars.

1931–1932 in Miniature

Through mail-order subscription, Danbury Mint (USA) offered a pewter 1931 dual-cowl phaeton in about 1⁄43 scale. Like all of the other cars in this series of classic cars, detail is fuzzy due to overpolishing. Collectors generally shy away from pewter models, for they seldom appreciate quickly, and their lack of color and flash make them less appealing to the eye.

French miniaturemaker Elegance specializes in hand-finished, ready-made, limited-production, museum-quality resin model Cadillacs. Some of its most noteworthy early miniatures issued during the 1980s were variations on the 1931 Series A V-16 chassis. Among the body styles offered were a convertible and a town car in 1⁄43 scale. These were produced in low volume, so they are seldom seen now and seldom resold. Since later Elegance models of more contemporary Cadillacs command several hundred dollars each, the early models are probably also well out of the financial ballpark of the casual collector.

If expensive limited editions are intimidating, the toy manufacturers offer lesser alternatives to model Cadillac collectors. Guisval of Spain offered an inexpensive 3¾" 1931 convertible coupe with metal body and plastic trim. Cute in two-tone paint, this mini-classic was intended for the playroom floor.

Very affordable, and needing only the patient hand of the model-kit builder, are lovely (and currently available) American Jo-Han 1⁄24-scale plastic kits of the snappy 1931 Series 452A V-16 two-seat cabriolet, the long and elegant Series 452A Fleetwood V-16 five-passenger phaeton, and the formal Series 452A Fleetwood V-16 town brougham. All three Jo-Han kits have beautifully detailed model engines, steerable wheels, and whitewalls. The cabriolet's rumble seat even operates! A talented modeler could conceivably cobble together a 1931 Indy pace car replica from a Jo-Han kit and Fred Cady aftermarket Indy pace car decals, but the V-16 engine would be incorrect. (Contact: Fred Cady Design, Inc., P.O. Box 576, Mt. Prospect, Illinois 60056.)

Canadian toy-carmaker Model Auto Emporium (MAE) also offers a pricey limited production 1⁄43-scale 1931 Series 452A V-16 boat-tailed speedster with option of top up (#114b) or down (#114a). The grille seems a bit on the chunky side, but other details and finish are museum quality. It is interesting to note that only one such real car was built, and it was painted in three successive color schemes — all offered on the MAE model: black, black and red, or pale blue and cream.

During the 1960s American model-kitmaker Pyro offered two easy-to-build 1⁄32-scale plastic 1931 Series A Cadillac kits — a town car and a sport phaeton. These kits never had a big following, so even though they have been out of production for some time, they show up with regularity at reasonable prices at collectors' shows.

The 1960s were good times for modelers who wanted to build the classics. Renwal created a whole series of tiny 1⁄48-scale polystyrene kits molded in glossy colors that eliminated the need for painting. One of the finest cars in this jewel-like series of great cars was a dark green and black 1931 dual-cowl phaeton. An added bonus to each of these delightful Lilliputian models in the series was a snap-together clear plastic display case. With the Renwal Caddy's fine but fragile details, this was the only way to protect the tiny phaeton from dust and clumsy finger-poking. Revell reissued the Cadillac (as well as a limited number of others from the Renwal Classic Series) in the late 1970s. Unfortunately, the nifty display cases were not included in any of the reissues, probably as a way to cut costs.

Italian die-cast miniaturemaker Rio still offers a green and black top-up (#76) and a gold and black top-down (#77) version of the Series 1931 Series A V-16 cabriolet in standard 1⁄43 scale. Rio seldom drops a number from its line of die-casts, so these are likely to be available for some years to come.

French die-cast miniature-carmaker Soldio now offers many custom or professional car-bodied versions of the 1931 Series 452A V-16 chassis. More common issues are the hearse, sedan delivery, ambulance, paddy wagon, fire department vehicle, and even an olive drab issue labeled a "U.S. Army Staff Car".

Verem, another French manufacturer, also offers a bizarre black and a white "Harlem Hearse" based on the same Solido die. One must remember that this body is an odd custom-coach style that might have been inspired by something built in Europe, for this was not a standard Cadillac offering. One wonders what the French must have been thinking about American commercial and fleet vehicles of the 1930s! Custom bodies on the durable and elegant Cadillac chassis were not uncommon, but a V-16 commercial delivery? Another notable variation was a special "gold"-plated gift-set version paired with a simulated pewter-finished 1957 Eldorado. Both were mounted on a red-flocked display stand with a stand-up sign that read "Centenary 1884-1984 par Solido".

A magnificent dark green 1932 Series 452B dual-cowl phaeton in 1⁄24 scale is available by mail-order subscription through the American Danbury Mint. Assembled in Hong Kong, this model is upholstered in soft leather and crowned with a delicate chromed heron radiator mascot. Wheels steer, and the V-16 engine is beautifully detailed under an authentic piano-hinged hood. A snap-on top-down boot or raised canvas-textured convertible roof is provided for display.

For those who do not want to pay the price of the Danbury Mint phaeton, American model-kitmaker Monogram offers a 1⁄24 scale 1932 phaeton plastic kit version with fewer working parts, but equally nice proportions and external trim detail.

1931

Danbury Mint (USA): Series 452A V-16 phaeton, 1⁄43, pewter; obsolete; less common. By subscription.
$35 – 90

Elegance (France): Series 452A V-16 convertible (top-down), 1⁄43, resin/handbuilt; obsolete; very rare. Expensive; low-production early Elegance model. **$200 – 450**

Top: *Boxed Jo-Han plastic kits for a 1931 two-seater cabriolet and V-16 phaeton.* ***Bottom:*** *1930 landaulette die-cast by Solido; pewter '31 phaeton offered by Danbury Mint (Ferd Zegel Collection); '31 convertible coupe made by Guisval; the Renwal/Revell plastic kit '31 phaeton; Rio die-cast '31 cabriolet (Ferd Zegel Collection).*

Elegance (France) d503: Series 452A V-16 town car, 1/43, resin/handbuilt; obsolete; very rare. Expensive; low-production early Elegance model. **$200 – 450**

Guisval (Spain): Series 452A V-16 convertible coupe, 3¾", crude metal/plastic toy; white body/black fenders; obsolete; less common. **$2 – 8**

Jo-Han (USA) GC-431: Series 452A V-16 two-seat cabriolet, 1/25, plastic kit, unpainted; current; common. **$5 – 17**

Jo-Han (USA) GC-131: Series 452A V-16 phaeton (open), 1/25, plastic kit, unpainted; current; common. **$5 – 17**

Jo-Han (USA) GC-731: Series 452A V-16 town brougham, 1/25, plastic kit, unpainted; current; common. **$5 – 17**

Model Auto Emporium (Canada) 114a: Series 452A V-16 boat-tail speedster, 1/43, die-cast; cream/blue, red/black, or black; current; less common. Expensive; limited current availability. **$175 – 250**

Model Auto Emporium (Canada) 114b: Series 452A V-16 boat-tail speedster (top-up), 1/43, die-cast; cream/blue, red/black, or black; current; less common. Expensive; limited current availability. **$175 – 250**

Pyro (USA) C-344: Series 452A V-16 sport phaeton, 1/32, plastic kit, unpainted; obsolete; less common. **$5 – 15**

Pyro (USA) C-346: Series 452A V-16 town car, 1/32, plastic kit, unpainted; obsolete; rare. **$5 – 15**

Renwal (USA) H1272: Series 452A V-16 dual-cowl phaeton (open), 1/48, plastic kit; green/black; obsolete; less common. Also available as a reissue of Renwal Classic Series done by Revell in the 1970s also. Revell reissue is impossible to tell from Renwal version. **$5 – 15**

Revell (USA): See Renwal, above.

Top: Solido die-casts and Pyro plastic kit of 1931 V-16s: U.S. Army staff car, town car, and fire chief car. ***Bottom:*** *Three uses of Solido dies: '31 "Coca-Cola" vehicle, sedan, and hearse.*

Rio (Italy) 76: Series A V-16 cabriolet (closed), 1⁄43, die-cast; green or black; current; common. **$8 – 30**

Rio (Italy) 77: Series A V-16 cabriolet (open), 1⁄43, die-cast; gold with black fenders; current; common. **$8 – 30**

Solido Golden Age (France) 85: Series 452A V-16 town car, 1⁄43, die-cast; black/beige, current; common. **$5 – 35**

Solido Golden Age (France) 4085: Series 452A V-16 town car, 1⁄43, die-cast; red or green; current; common. **$5 – 17**

Solido Golden Age (France): Series 452A V-16 1⁄43 die-cast professional/commercial body variations:

#404b hearse; current; common. **$5 – 17**

#407f sedan delivery "fan auto"; current; less common. **$5 – 50**

407h sedan delivery "Hewlett-Packard"; current; common. **$5 – 25**

#407Q sedan delivery "Queru"; current; common. **$5 – 25**

#4038 fire brigade/Manhattan chief's car; current; common. **$5 – 17**

#4042 ambulance/Denver, white; obsolete; less common. **$5 – 20**

#4043 police car, black; obsolete; less common. **$5 – 20**

#4057 police wagon; obsolete; less common. **$5 – 20**

#4060 sedan delivery "Cadbury"; current; common. **$5 – 17**

#4061 sedan delivery "Banania"; obsolete; less common. **$5 – 20**

#4065 sedan delivery "Waterman"; current; common. **$5 – 17**

#4066 sedan delivery "Coca-Cola"; current; common. **$5 – 35**

#4075 fire van "Sellers"; current; common. **$5 – 15**

#6003 U.S. Army staff car; current; common. **$5 – 17**

Solido Golden Age (France): hearse, 1⁄43, die-cast, gold body. Comes with pewter-finished '57 Eldorado in special "Centenary Set." **$15 – 50**

Verem (France): Series 452A professional/commercial body variations (from Solido molds and dies):

#306 hearse, 1⁄43, die-cast; black; current; common. **$5 – 25**

#307 Harlem hearse, 1⁄43, die-cast; white; current; common. **$5 – 25**

Handsome dark green V-16 sport phaeton, a die-cast 1/24-model available to Danbury Mint subscribers

1932

Danbury Mint (USA): Series 452B V-16 sport phaeton, 1/24, die-cast; dark green; current; common. Subscription purchase. **$40 – 80**

Monogram (USA) 2305: Series 452B V-16 phaeton, 1/25, plastic kit, unpainted; current; common. **$5 – 17**

1984-issue commemorative set from Solido containing "gold"-finished '31 V-16 and "pewter"-finished 1957 Eldorado

1933–1935

The Automobile

Stunning swept-back streamlining marked Cadillac and La Salle styling. Harley Earl's sleek 1933 Chicago World's Fair show car featured a rakishly slanted windshield, wind-cheating lines with voluptuous "pontoon" fenders, and an unusual fastback roof that forecast the new rounded styling trends to come in the late 1930s and into the 1940s. The nation's continuing economic woes caused V-16 sales to plummet. Sales of lesser Cadillacs also took away V-16 buyers, but the Depression was a miserable time for all carmakers. In 1933 combined Cadillac sales bottomed out at less than seven thousand cars. For a time there was talk of dropping the medium-priced La Salle, but Earl's masterful 1934 restyling gave the lovely La Salle new sales appeal and a reprieve from the corporate bean-counters' axe. And it was the third Cadillac product to set the pace at the Indy 500. By 1935 La Salle was fitted with an Oldsmobile straight-eight engine, a stamped-steel Fisher Body "Turret Top," independent front suspension, and new hydraulic brakes. Economic upturn was on the horizon, and Cadillac/La Salle sales began to improve.

Cadillac series numbers were changed for 1935. The V-8 Cadillac made up Series 10, 20, and 30; the V-12 was Series 40; and the V-16 was Series 60. The La Salle was the Cadillac division's lowest-priced offering, designated the Series 50.

1933–1935 in Miniature

California-based Entex model-kit distributors offered a large Japanese-made 1/16-scale plastic kit of the 1933 Series 452C V-16 town brougham for a brief time during the late 1970s. When completed, the big brougham duplicated the car once owned by movie star Joan Crawford. The engine sported simulated wiring, and the body included opening doors. The Entex kit was not overly expensive, but it was bulky when unbuilt in the carton. Consequently, few collectible-kit dealers like to tote one around to shows because of the large box.

However, a few might still languish unsold and unbuilt on dusty hobby shop shelves waiting to be bought.

Italeri (Italy) has recently released a pair of interesting 1933 Cadillacs in 1/25-scale kits to be distributed in the United States by Testors Corporation. Italeri is known for high-quality kits, and their Series 452C V-16 "all-weather phaeton" and "town car" continue the tradition.

In 1990 Matchbox International added a 1/43-scale 1933 Series 452C V-16 to their "Models of Yesteryear" series. Popularly priced, but slightly crude, this number is welcomed by Matchbox collectors.

England's Western Models makes a lovely medium-blue 1933 1/43-scale Series 452C dual-cowl phaeton in die-cast metal with raised top (#WM28). A companion piece is a burnt orange top-down version (#WM28X). The same number is also available in formal black. The gradual smoothing of Cadillac contours is easy to see in these fine models. Sadly, this model marked the final Fleetwood-bodied V-16 dual-cowl phaeton, and an era in open-air motoring ended.

Certainly one of the most desirable classic American die-cast toy cars is the Tootsietoy 1/48-scale 1934 La Salle. Crude by today's standards, the La Salle was a remarkable die-cast for its time. The Tootsietoy La Salles came in sets or separately, but only in two basic castings — a coupe (#0712, renumbered to #712 in 1937) and a sedan (#0713, renumbered to #713 in 1937). Some coupes had tops painted tan and were referred to as "convertible coupes" (#714, a simulated raised-top version?). Some sedans were also given the tan top treatment to be cataloged as "convertible sedans" (#715). La Salles had separate bright metal grilles and rode on solid white rubber tires on metal hubs. Collectors covet the Tootsietoy La Salles.

Buccaneer of England made copies of Tootsietoy La Salles in a softer "white" metal during the 1970s. Even though the Buccaneer copies were not made in huge numbers, they are still cheaper than the Tootsie originals. The most obvious difference between them is the plain unmarked chassis on the Buccaneer version. Dent (USA) also made a rare 1935 La Salle convertible, coupe, pickup truck, panel truck, and even a wrecker!

During the late 1970s Nostalgic Miniatures (USA) made a 1934 La Salle coupe. Modeled in pewter, it seems short, wide, and not particularly accurate. Rumor has it that a painted convertible (Indy pace car?) variation was available at one time also.

Young Cadillac model collectors might appreciate Mattel Hot Wheels' (made in both Malaysia and Hong Kong) 1935 Fleetwood V-12 town car. A number of color combinations are still available. Only the odd mag-wheel-style "Hot Wheels" spoil the effect of a nice inexpensive miniature in the pocket-sized 1/64 scale. This is a perfect starting model for very young Cadillac model collectors. A no-name copy of the Mattel car combines the body and fenders into a single metal casting, and details are very crude. In addition, garish stick-on flame decals (which are easily removable) mar an otherwise interesting variation on a theme.

1933

Entex (USA) 9029: Series 452C town brougham, 1/16, plastic kit, unpainted; obsolete; rare. **$25 – 100**

Italeri (Italy) 706: Series 452C V-16 Fleetwood "all-weather phaeton," 1/25, plastic kit, unpainted; current; common. Distributed by Testors Corp. in U.S. **$10 – 20**

Italeri (Italy) 707: Series 452C V-16 town car, 1/25, plastic kit, unpainted; current; common. Distributed by Testors Corp. in U.S. **$10 – 20**

Matchbox (GB) Y-34: Series 452C V-16 town car, 1/43, die-cast/plastic; dark blue; current; common. Models of Yesteryear Series. **$5 – 20**

Western (GB) WM28: Series 452C V-16 phaeton (top-up), 1/43, die-cast; blue; current; common. **$75 – 140**

Western (GB) WM28X: Series 452C V-16 phaeton (top-down), 1/43, die-cast; burnt orange or black; current; common. **$75 – 140**

1934

Buccaneer (GB): La Salle coupe, 1/48, "white" metal; obsolete; rare. 1970s reproduction of Tootsietoy La Salle sedan. **$25 – 45**

Nostalgic Miniatures (USA): La Salle coupe, 1/43, pewter; obsolete; rare. **$35 – 60**

Tootsietoy (USA) 0712 (renumbered 712 in 1937 catalog): La Salle coupe, 1/48, die-cast; obsolete; very rare. **$95 – 250**

Tootsietoy (USA) 0713 (renumbered 713 in 1937 catalog): La Salle sedan, 1/48, die-cast; obsolete; very rare. **$95 – 250**

Tootsietoy (USA 714: La Salle "convertible" coupe, 1/48, die-cast; tan roof; obsolete; very rare. Painted roof simulates convertible roof. **$95 – 250**

Tootsietoy (USA) 715: La Salle "convertible"sedan, 1/48, die-cast; tan roof (painted roof simulates convertible top); obsolete; very rare. Convertibles produced through 1936. **$95 – 250**

1935

Dent (USA): La Salle (sedan, coupe, open convertible, pickup, panel truck, wrecker), 1/48, cast-iron; obsolete; very rare. **$100 – 200**

Model of old-style gravity-feed gas pump (manufacturer unknown) nestled between Italeri plastic kits for a 1933 V-16 all-weather phaeton and a town car

Mattel Hot Wheels (Malaysia) 3252: Series 85 Fleetwood V-12 town car, 1/64, die-cast; current; common. Metal body/plastic fenders; "mag"-style wheels spoil effect.

$.50 – 2

Unknown (Hong Kong): Series 85 Fleetwood town car, 1/64, die-cast; red, with flame decals; current; common. Copy of Mattel with exception of one-piece body.

$.50 – 2

1937

The Automobile

With the auto market continuing a steady rebound, the elegant La Salle was once again upgraded. Gone was the straight-eight Olds engine, and in its place was a V-8 borrowed from the 1936 Series 60 Cadillac. Once again LaSalle paced the Indianapolis 500, this time with famed 1915 Indy winner Ralph DePalma at the wheel.

Refined styling and reduced prices raised sales. Even though La Salle still outsold Lincoln Zephyr, the low-line Packard beat it readily in the marketplace.

1937 in Miniature

In 1983 Jim Greenwood's Remarkable Replicas in West Chicago produced an all-new model of the 1937 La Salle in a style reminiscent of the great National Products models of the 1930s and 1940s. Smooth, cleanly molded, and an impressive 12" long, this 1/20-scale miniature La Salle was a nostalgic treat. While it felt much like the hefty pot metal used in the original National Products vehicle series, the Greenwood car was actually a much smoother composite of high-tech epoxy resin and aluminum

Top: *Two 1933 V-16s (Matchbox Models of Yesteryear die-cast town car and Western's die-cast Victoria); four 1934 La Salles (two are "white" metal Buccaneer reproductions of Tootsietoy's La Salles; next are a Tootsietoy sedan and a coupe) (both Ferd Zegel Collection); far right is a pewter coupe from Nostalgic Miniatures.* ***Bottom:*** *An unknown manufacturer's copy of a 1935 town car model by Mattel Hot Wheels is to the left of four color variations of the Mattel model.*

1934 La Salles: ***Top:*** *Tootsietoy's die-cast coupe and sedan.* ***Middle:*** *Buccaneer versions of Tootsietoy models — "white" metal coupe and a town car with a fanciful new body.* ***Bottom:*** *The La Salle coupe in pewter, from Nostalgic Miniatures.*

1937 La Salle coupe, as a magnificent model from Greenwood, sails past Cowdery Toy Works' Burma Shave signs.

powder. Today it could easily be mistaken for a fine styling model, with its silver opaque windows and careful masking of trim details.

Sadly, the production run of this lovely model was limited to a mere two hundred units — offered only in black, burgundy, or a handsome light yellow. At $125 in 1983, only serious collectors ever really got a shot at acquiring Greenwood's masterpiece. This is a gem.

1937

Greenwood (USA): La Salle coupe, 1/20, epoxy resin and aluminum powder; yellow, burgundy, or black; obsolete; rarest. Limited production. **$150 – 300**

1938–1940

The Automobile

Somehow Cadillac's V-16 car of kings had survived the Depression while many elite competitors withered and died. Demand for custom coachwork was at an all-time low. Even Packard turned away from its luxury tradition and sought sales in cheaper, less distinctive automobiles. In 1936 Cadillac embarked on its own cost-cutting program. The new Series 60 used standard Fleetwood bodies and a new V-8 that cast the crankcase and block as one very strong unit, making the venerable V-12 stone age by comparison. Fresh technology used in the new V-8 led to the development of a lighter short stroke V-16 that was less complex than earlier V-16s. The new super car-luxury model was unveiled at the 1937 New York Auto Show. However, the stock market took another beating shortly before the auto show, and the new V-16 never really found a niche in the comatose auto marketplace. Sadly, less than five hundred new V-16s were produced before being discontinued at the end of 1940 production. Carrying a V-16 line that would reflect favorably upon lesser V-8 Cadillacs (and even the entire GM line) offered some prestige value, but otherwise it had been a quirky business decision to introduce a new V-16 at all. Perhaps the expense was worth it in the long run — for the psychological marketing edge alone. History shows that when Packard abandoned the upper end of the luxury market, it never again recovered all of its coveted prestige.

Newcomer William Mitchell was credited for the grand styling of 1938 Cadillacs and La Salles. Twenty years later, the talented Mitchell would assume Harley Earl's mantle at GM. Both Earl and Mitchell created a striking blend of futuristic and traditional design. Even traditional side-mounted spare tires looked pleasingly sleek and modern on Mitchell's designs and proved to be popular options. Although some of the new all-steel bodies even shared some sheet metal between series to save cost, the V-16 was still king of the road; its pulling power and smoothness were unmatched. Perhaps this legendary performance was the reason that mobster Al Capone chose a 1940 V-16 for personal transport at his residence in Miami. In addition, two V-16s with special stretched bodies served in the White House motor pool during the FDR era. But by 1940, the big V-16 custom-bodied super cars went the way of the dinosaur: suddenly, they were gone in a whisper.

Another 1940 loss was the La Salle. Although the car was continually refined and restyled, the lovely La Salle never could compete in sales with the low-line Packard. In addition, sister Buick division also worried that La Salle cut into its sales. A shrinking market at the top of the medium-priced field finally prompted Cadillac management to kill the La Salle and let the Series 61 Cadillac take up the sales slack as an entry-level offering.

1938–1940 in Miniature

The least accurate model of a 1938 Series 90 town car is not a model at all but a two-piece "gold"-plated bottle by Avon for aftershave lotion (pictured in the Introduction to this book). The bottle's function dictates that its detail is (at best) vague. A huge rear section that roughly follows the contours of the trunk unscrews for access to the liquid contents. Most model collectors will probably pass on this impressionistic "collectible."

Brooklin Models of England makes a 1940 Series 90 two-door convertible coupe that comes painted in flawless metallic brown with flat beige simulated raised convertible roof. Toys For Collectors, a popular Massachusetts toy dealer, had a limited number made (in the same color as the regular issue) with a cast top-down boot. The ultimate Brooklin variation is the special red-painted version (with side-mounted spares) prepared by Brooklin for the annual Canadian Toy Show in 1983. Brooklin Collectors continue to drive the price of this rare red version up into the stratosphere.

Tom Mills of TKM Models of Oklahoma cast a whole line of 1/25-scale model Cadillacs in resin and sold them by direct mail order. These models were not as easy to assemble as the plastic-model kits available at the hobby shop, for they demanded a great deal of handwork and careful finishing. Quality varied between issues and individual castings, but such cottage-industry sources are valuable in helping fill gaps between the offerings of the big model and toy companies. Mills made a 1938 Series 75 town car and a 1939 Series 60 sedan. Nobody else has offered 1/25-scale models of these cars.

Canada's Model Auto Emporium currently offers resin 1/43-scale Series 60 Specials with or without side-mounted spares. These are disappointing models for their high prices. MAE has done better work.

Rextoys of Switzerland worked with Fulgarex (of metal-model kit fame) to create a die-cast line of 1/43-scale replicas of the 1938-1940 Series 90 V-16 Cadillacs in various body styles. In fact, Rextoys is still adding variations of color and body configurations. Among its offerings at this writing are a Cadillac V-16 papal limousine with figures of Pope Pius XII and his drivers, a V-16 town car (upholstered roof with open driver compartment), a V-16 closed limousine (upholstered roof), and a V-16 formal sedan in a series of three American military staff cars that share the same basic serial number (#04). The V-16 U.S. Army staff car is olive drab with white markings. The U.S. Army Air Force staff car carries 1944 USAAF Europe markings on its bumpers. The last staff car is the U.S. Navy version in light blue. A V-16 two-door sports coupe is #05 while #06 is a V-16 two-door convertible with top down. Rextoys also offers a celebrity version of the V-16 top-down convertible coupe — in pink — with a barely clad figure of porn star/Italian parliament member Ciccolina lounging in the back seat. Whimsical! For those who like big open convertibles, #0012 is a four-door convertible sedan with top down. An interesting variation on this four-door convertible model is #0012R, a special version with presidential flags and a

Versions of the V-16 of 1938. ***Top:*** *Rextoy's die-cast four-door convertible sedan and sports coupe (both Ferd Zegel Collection).* ***Middle:*** *The Pope Pius XII limousine by Rextoy.* ***Bottom:*** *Special version, for Italian film star Ciccolina, and the more subdued convertible coupe, made by Rextoy.*

figure of President Franklin D. Roosevelt as a distinguished passenger.

Hubley (USA) made a crude 7"-long 1940 La Salle sedan with white rubber tires and separate nickel-plated grille and headlight pods. This is a seldom-seen toy that came in both sedan and taxi versions and now commands a healthy price at collector shows.

Mikansue Models of England makes a line of "white" metal kits that often fills large gaps in auto history but usually at the expense of fine detail. Its 1940 La Salle sedan commemorates the last year of La Salle production. Unfortunately, Mikansue kits have spotty availability unless one has connections in England, where "white" metal kit building is high sport.

1938–1940

(*Note*: A span of years is used here since there were few differences between the Cadillacs produced then and some manufacturers did not differentiate among their models for 1938-1940.)

Avon (USA): 1938 Series 90 town car, 7¼", glass after-shave bottle, gold-plated; obsolete; less common.
$1 – 10

Brooklin (GB) 14: 1940 Series 90 V-16 two-door convertible coupe (top-up), 1⁄43, die-cast; metallic brown/beige top; current; common. **$30 – 70**

Brooklin (GB) 14: 1940 Series 90 V-16 two-door convertible (top-down); 1⁄43, die-cast; metallic brown/beige top; obsolete; rare. This version was done for "Toys for Collectors." **$45 – 125**

Brooklin (GB) 14: 1940 convertible coupe, 1⁄43, die-cast; red; obsolete; very rare. Special limited-production 1983 Canadian Toy Show version with side mounts.
$100 – 350

Hubley (USA): 1940 La Salle sedan, 7", die-cast; obsolete; very rare. Separate nickel-plated grille and headlight pods. **$150 – 350**

Other 1938 V-16s. ***Top:*** *U.S. Navy and U.S. Army Air Force staff cars, and a sedan, die-cast by Rextoy.* ***Bottom:*** *Brooklin's standard issue and its special 1983 Canadian Toy Show issue with fender-mounted spare tire (Ferd Zegel Collection).*

Seven-inch 1940 La Salle, die-cast by Hubley (Ferd Zegel Collection)

Miniatures of President Franklin D. Roosevelt and drivers distinguish this Rextoys variation of the V-16 four-door convertible.

Mikansue (GB): 1940 La Salle sedan, 1/43, "white" metal kit; obsolete; less common. **$20 – 40**

Model Auto Emporium (Canada) 117: Series 60 Special four-door sedan, 1/43, factory-built resin kit; two-tone green; current; less common. **$100 – 200**

Model Auto Emporium (Canada) 117a: Series 60 Special four-door sedan, 1/43, factory-built resin kit; two-tone blue; current; less common. **$100 – 200**

Model Auto Emporium (Canada) 117b: Series 60 Special, two-door coupe, 1/43, factory-built resin kit; green; current; less common. **$100 – 200**

Rextoys (Switzerland) 01: V-16 town car, 1/43, die-cast; black; current; common. Special version; Pope Pius XII car. **$17 – 35**

Rextoys (Switzerland) 02: V-16 town car, 1/43, die-cast; current; common. By Fulgarex. **$17 – 35**

Rextoys (Switzerland) 03: V-16 closed limousine, 1/43, die-cast; current; common. Simulated upholstered roof. **$17 – 35**

Rextoys (Switzerland) 04a: V-16 formal sedan/U.S. Army staff car, 1/43, die-cast; olive drab; current; common. **$17 – 35**

Rextoys (Switzerland) 04af: V-16 formal sedan/U.S. Army Air Force staff car, 1/43, die-cast; current; common. **$17 – 35**

Rextoys (Switzerland) 04n: V-16 formal sedan/U.S. Navy staff car, 1⁄43, die-cast; current; common. **$17 – 35**

Rextoys (Switzerland) 05: V-16 sports coupe, 1⁄43, die-cast; current; common. **$17 – 35**

Rextoys (Switzerland) 06: V-16 convertible (top-down), 1⁄43, die-cast; current; common. **$17 – 35**

Rextoys (Switzerland) 07: V-16 convertible (top-down), 1⁄43, die-cast; current; common. Special pink version with figures of Ciccolina and driver. **$17 – 40**

Rextoys (Switzerland) 12: V-16 four-door convertible (top-down), 1⁄43, die-cast; current; common. **$17 – 35**

Rextoys (Switzerland) 12R: V-16 four-door convertible (top-down), 1⁄43, die-cast; current; common. Special dark blue version with figures of President Roosevelt and drivers. **$17 – 45**

TKM (USA): 1938 Series 75 town car, 1⁄25, resin kit, unpainted; less common. **$15 – 35**

TKM (USA): 1939 Series 60 sedan, 1⁄25, resin kit, unpainted; less common. **$15 – 35**

1941–1942

The Automobile

The world was a different place by 1940. War clouds were gathering, and automotive industry leaders realized it was only a matter of time before strategic materials would be needed by the government, and factories would be diverted from automobile production. Cadillac generated a full head of steam for its 1940 to 1942 efforts before the storm of World War II finally broke.

The Art and Color Studios juggled body styles and smoothed and refined an already fine product for 1940, but Cadillac would have to outdo itself to replace the prestige lost when the custom luxury body trade melted away and the spectacular V-16 was finally dropped. At the other end of the market, even the La Salle was no longer offered in the division's line.

The strikingly new 1941 Cadillac was just the last hurrah that was needed before America entered World War II. Headlights became part of streamlined fenders, and the trademark Cadillac "egg-crate" grille appeared for the first time. Elegant, aloof, yet sporty in a massive way, the 1941 Cadillac exceeded all expectations of public and GM management alike. It was a runaway sales success. After a mildly restyled 1942 model was introduced, only about 5,000 cars were built before Cadillac turned from auto production to tank and aircraft engine production for World War II.

1941–1942 in Miniature

The 1941-1942 Cadillac is not represented in great numbers in scale models. Tom Mill's TKM Models offered a resin kit of the 1941 Series 62 convertible and the 1941 Series 60 Special in 1⁄25 scale. Both required much handwork, but the TKM models were faithful to the lines of the cars.

Wyandotte Toys (USA) made a large (over 20" long!) pressed-steel custom-bodied Series 61 "woody" station wagon. Cadillac trim and bumpers were lithographed on the sheet steel body, and back doors were hinged on fragile metal tabs so junior could stash his building blocks or frog collection in the spacious igloolike body. Although the big Wyandotte surfaces with some regularity at toy shows, it is difficult to find a complete one with doors intact.

Lastly, Hubley offered a 7"-long 1942 Series 62 sedan in die-cast metal. Interestingly enough, Hubley even grafted a taxi roof light on one variation! Most all of these cars rolled on black rubber wheels and wore odd two-tone paint jobs. Some even had lithographed sheet-metal chassis. Hubley cranked out toys in great number, so the Hubley '42 is not exceptionally rare.

1941

TKM (USA): Series 62 convertible, 1⁄25, resin kit, unpainted; obsolete; less common. **$20 – 30**

TKM (USA): Series 60 Special, 1⁄25, resin kit, unpainted; obsolete; less common. **$20 – 30**

Wyandotte (USA): Coachcraft Custom Estate "woody" wagon, 1⁄12, lithographed pressed steel; red or blue; obsolete; very rare (for a complete one). Passenger doors open and are frequently broken. **$75 – 250**

1942

Hubley (USA): Series 62 sedan, 7", metal; obsolete; rare. Taxi version also available. **$45 – 150**

1941 convertible, a resin kit by TKM

Wyandotte's pressed-steel 1941 Coachcraft Custom Estate "woody" station wagon; also available as a "sedan delivery" commercial version (Ferd Zegel Collection)

POST–WORLD WAR II PRODUCTION 1946–1976

1946–1949

The Automobile

Cadillac ended war production and resumed auto production for 1946. Since the 1942 Cadillac line was new when factories changed over to war work in 1942, there was little incentive to change it significantly for the 1946 and 1947 Cadillacs. The postwar era was a sellers' market anyway, so new products would be better timed for when the market softened and pent-up consumer demand began to ease. Cadillac stylists used this time to gear up for the new generation of post–World War II models to debut in 1948.

In 1948 Cadillac began introducing a string of styling features that would change the shape of the American automobile for years to come. In 1939 Harley Earl had seen an early example of the GM-Allison-powered Lockheed P-38 Lightning fighter plane at a military airfield near Detroit. The sweeping lines and supercharger power bulges in the exotic twin-boomed fuselage captured Earle's imagination. Soon the Art and Color Section at GM was buzzing with activity to combine the aero look into design studies for postwar GM cars. Wraparound cockpits, air scoops, pontoon fenders, and wind-cheating noses were tried, tweaked, and modified. The P-38's twin rudders inspired the tail fins that Cadillac pioneered in 1948, giving Cadillacs a unique styling motif that survives in vestigial form to this day. It was a masterstroke of production design that spawned a sea full of imitators.

The 1949 Cadillac continued the knockout styling themes introduced in 1948 and added a new hardtop at mid-year that quickly became the most popular body style of all — the Coupe de Ville. With the power of its all-new 331-cid high-compression ohv V-8 engine that could utilize the higher octane motor fuels newly available after World War II, there were few machines on the road that could match the Cadillac's performance.

1946–1949 in Miniature

One of the most interesting Cadillac miniatures from this era was the Auburn Rubber 1⁄43-scale postwar Cadillac styling study dream car done in red with airbrushed silver trim. It seemed to be a composite of the styling features showcased by Cadillac in a series of ads and publicity pictures promising futuristic cars to come. Such studies were only a taste of the Motorama styling dream cars to debut in the 1950s. Auburn rubber toy cars are not particularly rare today, but finding one in good shape is not always that easy.

Marx toymakers jumped on the toy Cadillac bandwagon by offering a 6¼" plastic-bodied 1949 coupe with wooden wheels. Detail is minimal, but the P-38-inspired rear fender tips are Cadillac. Some

Harley Earl was inspired by the twin-tail design of the P-38, and the result was the famous 1948 Cadillac tail fin (Lockheed Photo).

1947 Series 62. ***Top:*** *Four-door sedan and two-door sedanette, Provence Moulage resin kits.* ***Bottom:*** *Convertible and two-door sedanette, Tron factory-built resin models.*

collectors speculate that this crude car was probably cargo on a Marx auto-carrier set.

TKM listed a 1946 and 1947 Series 62 coupe as well as a 1947 convertible in 1/25-scale resin kit form that had to be assembled and painted.

Tron Club of Italy offers a handbuilt 1/43 resin model of the natty 1947 Series 62 convertible as well as a fastback coupe, painted in authentic Cadillac two-tone schemes. Tiny emblems are recreated by decals and metal foil. These models are museum quality, and they are priced accordingly.

Provence Moulage of France also offers a 1/43-scale resin version of the 1947 Series 62 coupe — but in kit form. Details are good, and a skilled modeler can make a model as nice as the Tron coupe at a fraction of Tron's price. The Provence Moulage kit even captures the subtleties of the fastback body lines better. Provence Moulage also offers convertible and sedan companion pieces in the same material and scale.

The Danish toymaker Joker was one of several small manufacturers that grew up after World War II. Unfortunately, like many of these companies, Joker did not survive the early 1950s. However, Joker did die-cast a crude 6" 1947 Series 62 sedanette. It featured a tin baseplate and rubber tires on cast-metal wheels. Joker toys were not distributed in America.

1946 styling dream car, in rubber by Auburn

Ralstoy, an American company mainly known for its simple metal promotional toy trucks, produced a roughly 1/43-scale stylized 1947 Cadillac sedan toy and marketed it through the Woolworth dime stores for Christmas of 1948. It first appeared in various colors. However, it was a dismal sales failure. In 1949 Ralstoy remarketed it, only this time they had an Omaha plating shop chrome plate the body. The shiny new model was a hit! By fall of 1949 plating shops all around the Omaha area were plating Ralstoy Cadillacs as fast as they could to satisfy the

1948 Cadillac 60 Specials. ***Top:*** *Regular and economy HO-scale die-cast models from Mercury.* ***Bottom:*** *Tootsietoy die-casts.*

Joker's 1947 Series 62 sedanette (Ferd Zegel Collection)

demand for what had been a major dog only a year before. The mystery is that although the Ralstoy 1947 Cadillac was turned out in large numbers, it is rarely seen today. Where did all of the Ralstoy Cadillacs go?

Modeler John Boehm (USA) kit-bashed AMT 1950 Chevrolet bodies into rough approximations of the 1948 Cadillac in coupe, convertible, and fastback sedanette body configurations and then cast the bodies in fiberglass resin to sell to fellow modelers. Numbers on these "conversions" were very low, although word has it that many castings found their way to Europe in the last few years when collectors over there suddenly rediscovered American cars.

Mercury of Italy created two 1948 Cadillac 60 Specials. The first was a 1⁄43-scale die-cast with separate bare-metal bumpers that were part of the baseplate casting. Unfortunately, these bumpers were very fragile, and unbroken versions are hard to find now. Poor paint and even metal fatigue are common. A pity, for although the model lacked an interior, its lines were unmistakably Cadillac and very pleasing. A companion piece, possibly intended as an HO railroad accessory, was a 2¼" pantographed copy of the larger 1⁄43-scale model. Because of its diminutive size, the bumpers were not cast separately, and the metal wheels were painted body color. The smaller Mercury Cadillac is not as scarce today as the larger 1⁄43 version, although Mercury models never enjoyed widespread distribution in the United States.

Chicago-based Tootsietoy made a 6" 1948 60 Special sedan that was listed in its sales catalogs for many years. Because of the type of axle used to hold the wheels in place, the front and rear wheels were necessarily skirted. This was odd, but the long narrow toy has the egg-crate grille and P-38-style rear fender tips that are obviously Cadillac. The Tootsietoy was in wide distribution for many years, but the ones with less play wear will command higher prices.

In the late 1970s movie-prop maker/skilled modeler Marty Martino was experimenting with different casting

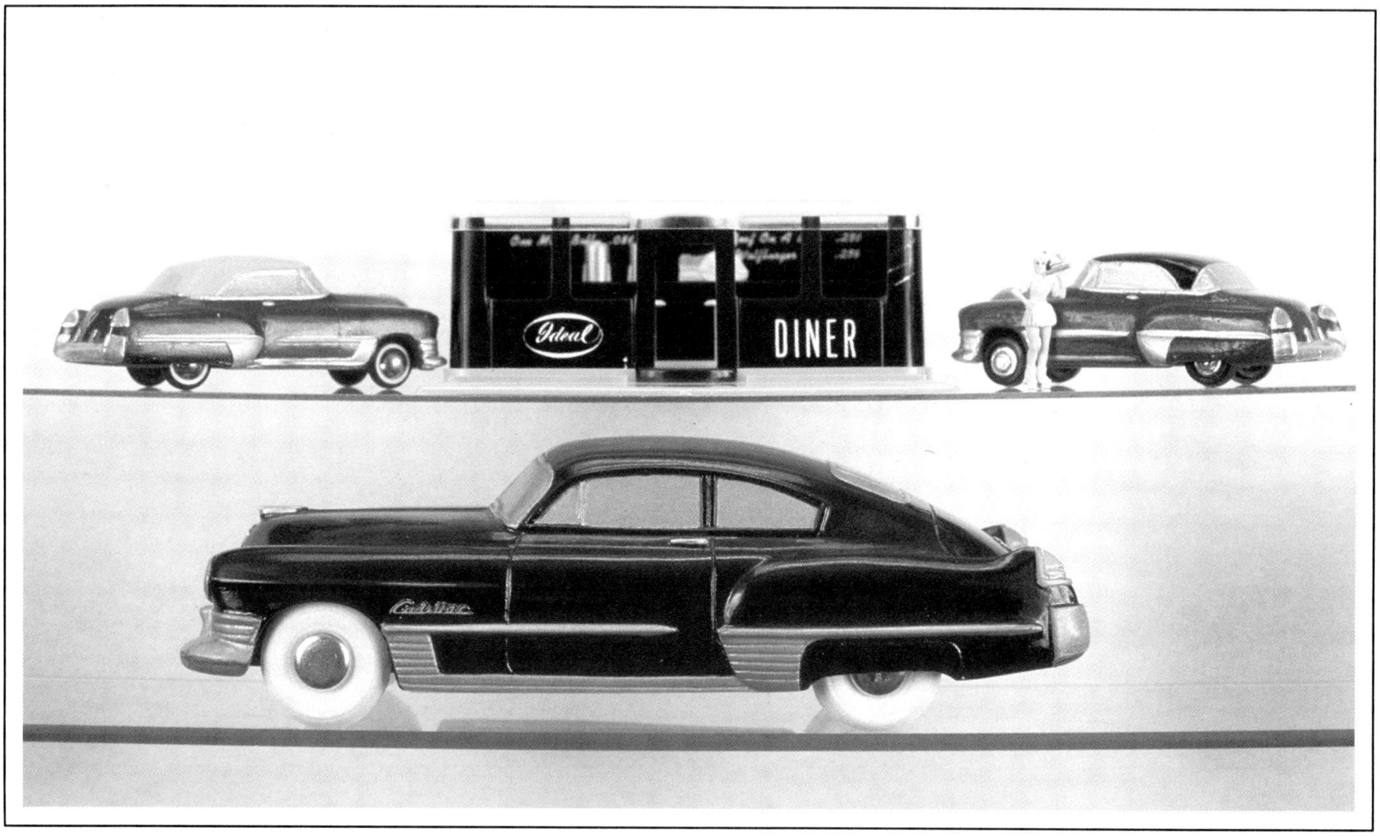

Top: *Martino's 1949 Series 62 convertible and coupe pull up to an Ideal diner.* ***Bottom***: *Epoxy and aluminum powder composite created by Martino to represent a large 1/18-scale sedanette of the same vintage.*

materials for a limited production run of less than ten 1949 miniature Cadillacs taken directly from two scratch-built originals. Close to 1/40 scale, these charming, solid-cast, tiny hardtops and convertibles are probably closer to auto folk art than scale models. The convertible (modeled with raised top) was cast in hard amber resin while the coupe is cast in plaster. Martino used a variety of media — including the patching compound used in furnace repair! Nearly a decade later, in 1987, Martino created a larger 1/18-scale 1949 Series 62 sedanette in "cold-cast" metal (a mixture of epoxy resin and aluminum powder); it was #1 in his "Route 66" series of models. Most of Marty Martino's work is limited production, and the hefty 11½" cold-cast model is no exception. Available only in black or maroon, the model was limited to a production of one hundred. With solid silver windows and masked silver trim, the Martino Cadillac resembles a styling studio model. Early examples have soft white silicone rubber tires and no metal baseplate. Later versions have hard white resin tires and a steel baseplate with Martino's signature, the series number, and date. Not many collectors even got a shot at this beauty.

1949 sedanette, as a resin kit from TKM

1949 Lapin plastic Cads. ***Top:*** *Convertible and sedan, plastic service station island with Shell gas pumps (manufacturer unknown).* ***Bottom:*** *Larger version of above sedan.*

TKM offered a 1⁄25-scale resin kit of the 1948 Series 62 sedanette and 1949 Series 62 convertible. Casting was crude, but collectors are forgiving when a less than perfect model is one of the few available. Tom Mills chose his subjects well. Model collectors owe him a debt.

A tin drive-in roadside playset, complete with plastic carhops, yielded two simple but pleasing 1949 Cadillac toys by Lapin (USA). The first was a 6" plastic Series 61 sedan of cartoonish proportions with white plastic snap-in wheels. The second Lapin was a clone of sorts, for it was similar to the sedan, except that the top was removed to make a four-door convertible. A basic interior tub (without dash or steering wheel) completed the convertible effect. Still other variations were larger 8¾" pantographed copies of the Lapin 6" sedan and convertible. These were nice, brightly colored toys that were never intended to be scale models, and they should be appreciated for their simple play value.

1946

Auburn (USA): styling dream car, 1⁄43, rubber; usually red; obsolete; rare. **$20 – 35**

TKM (USA): Series 62 coupe, 1⁄25, resin kit, unpainted; obsolete; less common. **$20 – 35**

1947

Joker (Denmark): Series 62 sedanette, 6", mixed metal; obsolete; very rare. Crude and seldom seen. **$15 – 50**

Provence Moulage (France): Series 62 two-door convertible, 1⁄43, resin kit, unpainted; current; less common. **$20 – 35**

Provence Moulage (France): Series 62 two-door fastback, 1⁄43, resin kit, unpainted; current; less common. **$20 – 35**

Provence Moulage (France): Series 62 four-door sedan, 1⁄43, resin kit, unpainted; current; less common. **$20 – 35**

Ralstoy (USA): generic sedan, about 1⁄43, die-cast toy; obsolete; rare. High production but apparently low survival rate. **$10 – 35**

TKM (USA): Series 62 coupe, 1⁄25, resin kit, unpainted; obsolete; less common. **$20 -35**

TKM (USA): Series 62 convertible, 1⁄25, resin kit, unpainted; obsolete; less common. **$20 – 35**

Tron (Italy) 6: Series 62 convertible, 1⁄43, factory-built resin kit; yellow; current; less common. **$80 – 180**

Tron (Italy) 10: Series 62 fastback, 1⁄43, factory-built resin kit; current; less common. Low production, high price. **$80 – 180**

1948

Boehm (USA): convertible, 1⁄25, resin kit, unpainted; obsolete; rare. Resin conversions from AMT 1950 Chevy kits (done about 1977). **$15 – 35**

Boehm (USA): coupe, 1⁄25, resin kit, unpainted; obsolete; rare. Resin conversions from AMT 1950 Chevy kits (done about 1977). **$15 – 35**

Boehm (USA): sedanette, 1⁄25, resin kit, unpainted; obsolete; rare. Resin conversions from AMT 1950 Chevy kits (done about 1977). **$15 – 30**

Mercury (Italy): Series 60 Special, HO, die-cast; obsolete; rare. These seem more plentiful than 1⁄43 version, below. **$10 – 30**

Mercury (Italy): Series 60 Special, 1⁄43, die-cast; obsolete; rare. Delicate bumpers, crude greenhouse. **$70 – 175**

Tootsietoy (USA): Series 60 Special four-door sedan, 6", die-cast; obsolete; rare (when in good condition). Difficult to find not playworn. **$12 – 45**

1949

Lapin (USA): convertible, 6", plastic toy; obsolete; less common. **$5 – 15**

Lapin (USA): four-door convertible, 8¾", plastic toy; obsolete; less common. **$5 – 15**

Three Cadillac coupes. ***Top:*** *1950 model, vinyl from Alskog Design; Marx's 1949 coupe in plastic.* ***Bottom:*** *Wyandotte's plastic 1950 models.*

Lapin (USA): sedan, 6", plastic toy; obsolete; less common. **$5 – 15**

Lapin (USA): sedan, 8¾", plastic toy; obsolete; less common. **$5 – 15**

Martino Miniatures (USA): Series 62 convertible, 5", crude unpainted plaster; obsolete; rarest. Limited production. **$45 – 75**

Martino Miniatures (USA): Series 62 hardtop, 5", unpainted plaster; obsolete; rarest. Limited production. **$45 – 75**

Martino Miniatures (USA) 1: Series 62 sedanette fastback, 1⁄18, mixture of epoxy resin and aluminum powder; black or maroon; obsolete; rare. Low production (100). **$90 – 180**

Marx (USA): Series 62 coupe, 6¼", plastic; obsolete; less common. Wooden wheels. **$5 – 15**

TKM (USA): Series 62 convertible, 1⁄25, resin kit, unpainted; obsolete; less common. **$20 – 35**

1950

The Automobile

Cadillac seemed to be able to give the country just what it needed and wanted in a luxury car during the 1950s, and it was reluctant to change a winning line-up. Styling changes for 1950 were understandably few as America moved boldly into the atomic age. The curved, one-piece windshield replaced the 1949 split affair, and the holdover Series 75 limousine based on the old 1941-1947 body was finally restyled to match the other models in the line. Bigger was better, and chrome was the automotive sculptor's medium.

The ohv V-8, introduced only a year before, gave Cadillac a new performance image. Cadillacs even swept two classes in the Grand Canyon Mobilgas economy run when professional drivers coaxed an incredible 27 miles per gallon from their Cadillac V-8 engines. Automotive publications also gushed over the Series 61 coupe as America's fastest production car! Cadillac's V-8 was *the* hot set-up that racers sought for speed and bulletproof reliability above all others of the day. Southern California hotrodders regularly turned out Fordillac and Studellac conversions to wipe the competition at drag races. Flushed with success in his initial outing in a Cadillac-powered Healy, famed sportsman Briggs Cunningham modified two 1950 Cadillacs to compete at the grueling but prestigious French 24-hour race at Le Mans.

The most modified of the two Cunningham Cadillac racers was a huge, rebodied, slab-sided, "aerodynamic," open roadster dubbed "Le Monstre" by the French because of the car's strange aircraft carrier-like appearance. The blue and white lightweight (?) roadster was blindingly fast, powerful, and unlucky. On the Sunday before the race, while trying to impress a female passenger, team driver Phil Walters accidentally rammed a farmer's hay wagon on the rural French roads that serve as the Le Mans race course. Fortunately, no one was hurt, but "Le Monstre" was badly bent. Frantic to make the race, the Cunningham racing team quickly chartered a private plane to rush aluminum body expert Bob Blake from England in a desperate last-minute effort to repair the extensive damage. A day and a half of nonstop body knocking put "Le Monstre" back in shape for pre-race inspection.

Unfortunately, the Cunningham Special's problems were not over. During Briggs Cunningham's turn behind the wheel early in the race, "Le Monstre" skittered off the course on a corner and wedged deep into a sandbank. Valuable time was lost digging out. The powerful Cadillac V-8 engine enabled the crippled machine to make up much lost time, but then the lower transmission gears gave out. Despite having to drive only in high gear for the remainder of the race, drivers Walters and Cunningham brought "Le Monstre" home to a remarkable eleventh-place finish. Not bad at all for a car that seemed plagued with bad luck.

Although the "Le Monstre" story is a tale of courage and determination, it is only half the story of the Cunningham team's epic struggle to win the 1950 Le Mans race. The open roadster's sister car deserves more than casual mention, for it was a race-tweaked but otherwise very stock Series 61 coupe dubbed "Petit Petaud." In fact, waggish drivers Miles and Sam Collier even wore business suits and neckties while piloting their very stock-looking competition Cad around the Le Mans track at a blistering pace to a tenth-place finish — one slot ahead of the thundering "Le Monstre"! Shades of the Blues

Brothers! Cunningham was encouraged by his success with his competition Cadillac team, and he returned to America to begin construction of a line of Cunningham sports cars that he hoped would one day win the Le Mans race for his country.

The remarkable Cunningham saga was not the only Cadillac success story at Le Mans in 1950. Sydney Allard and Tom Cole drove a Cadillac-powered Allard J-2 (with only top gear still working by the end of the race) and managed a third-place finish.

Sydney Allard's remarkable, cycle-fendered, Cadillac-powered J-2X was one of the most rip-roaring competition roadsters of the early 1950s, with a string of remarkable racing victories to its credit.

Sydney Allard was a successful British Ford dealer in London, and he experimented with V-8 Ford engines in his odd-looking cycle-fendered J-1 racers. The light but fast Allards embarrassed many a Jag and Ferrari in competition and gained a loyal following.

Clever engineering allowed the J-2 Allard roadsters to be fitted with a variety of rugged American Mercury, Chrysler, and — most importantly — Cadillac V-8 drive trains. The Anglo-American hybrids amazed and terrified race watchers with their bellowing power and strange split-front axle geometry that pointed the wheels in all manner of strange ways. The body was prone to flex, and the primitive door latches would often allow the doors to fly open on sharp turns! Driving this open-cockpit road rocket was not for the faint of heart, and wearing a seat belt, as well as a kidney belt, was mandatory. Legendary drivers Erwin Goldschmidt and Larry Pomeroy literally wrestled their flying Allards to victory again and again.

Modifications to the J-2's spooky split-front suspension produced the J-2X, and this Caddy-powered monster could streak from rest to 100 mph in a mere dozen seconds. Dated and quirky chassis or not, it was a long time before the competition could finally eclipse the Cad-Allard's formidable record of performance and durability. Carroll Shelby acknowledged that the inspiration for his rip-roaring AC Cobra of the 1960s was the powerful V-8 Allard.

Cadillac's role in the Korean War rearmament program caused the supply of Cadillac V-8s to dry up suddenly. Hotrodders and racers had to find other sources of high-performance engines, and the powerful new Chrysler "Hemi" became the successor to the racing throne as much by default as by virtue of its fine design.

1950 in Miniature

America's automotive symbol of success for 1950 was a popular choice for toys and models.

1950 die-cast convertible, AMR kit

1950 coupe in tin, by unknown manufacturer

Arcor rubber Series 62 coupe

1950 coupe de pencil box, made in tin by Beetland

Rare, expensive, handmade resin model from Elegance: 1950 Series 75 limousine

Swedish toymaker Alskog Design molded a 1950 Cadillac coupe in soft vinyl for the playpen trade. Its wide snap-in wheels were more suited to an off-road vehicle (but then one wonders how many real 1950 Cadillacs could there be to use as patterns in Sweden?). The Alskog Caddie is also mislabeled a 1947 on the underside.

French model manufacturer AMR made a fine "white" metal kit, marked a Series 61 convertible, that can become museum quality in the hands of a talented modeler. A companion piece and variation was the AMR Cunningham Le Mans coupe, apparently cast from the same mold, with a roof added. The Cunningham racer version does not have the stock convertible's plated bumpers and trim, leading one to believe that the competition coupe was part of a lesser "economy" line of kits.

Hard-rubber toy vehicles lost popularity in the 1950s with the advent of new plastics, but Arcor Safe-Play Toys made a 1/32-scale hard rubber Series 62 Sedan with odd skirted front wheels and painted silver windows and trim. This was a hardy toy intended for long tours of the playroom floor by young Cadillac fans. Rubber toys were and are durable, but it is often difficult to find a fine example that has not warped and/or dried out by now (after forty-plus years).

Beetland, noted distributor of pop-culture gift items, sold a 7¾" pressed-tin pencilbox that vaguely resembles a 1950 Cadillac coupe. All windows, side trim, grille, and bumpers are silkscreened on the basic box form that splits to open at the beltline. Cute, but hardly a precision miniature.

During the 1980s Elegance of France built a reputation — and loyal following of collectors — by creating a series of high-priced, high-quality, 1/43-scale, resin Cadillac models that collectors covet. Variations on a theme are dizzying. Among these jewels of the modeler's art are a Series 75 limousine, a Series 75 Derham seven-passenger sedan, a Series 62 two-door coupe, a Series 60 Special four-door sedan, a Series 62 four-door sedan, a Series 86 New York City fire ambulance, a Series 86 ambulance, a Series 86 funeral hearse, a Series 86 funeral service car, and a Series 75 Derham four-door limousine. Collectors are lucky to add even one of these beautifully finished models

1950 Series 62 coupe in resin, from Elegance. A handmade jewel. Note French-style yellow headlight lens.

1950 Series 62 coupes, in FIFTIES pressed steel. ***Top:*** *This is distinguished as an early series car with no Cadillac script on front fenders or red hubcap center.* ***Bottom:*** *A second series car, with script and red hubcap center.*

This 1950 Series 62 convertible is also a second series car, with script, from FIFTIES; Mary Kay's delight in pink.

*Compare the FIFTIES pressed-steel 1950 Series 62 coupe **(top)** with the Luxe Car **(below)**. The Chinese-made copy is roughly made, with crude stamping, different hood mascot, and plain hubcaps.*

to their collections. And at several hundred dollars per model, few collectors are committed enough to collect all variations.

FIFTIES (Japan) set the toy-collecting world on its collective ear in the mid-1980s with the release of an entirely new 1⁄18-scale pressed-steel ("tin" to collectors) 1950 Series 62 convertible and coupe reminiscent of the highly prized Japanese Marusan toy Cadillacs made during the Eisenhower years. These were not exact copies of the Marusan cars at all, for the masters were created by skilled Japanese mold maker/wood carver Masao Sugiyama (a septuagenarian toy buff himself). The Caddy was the first in a series of beautiful factory-finished toy cars that included a '50 Buick, '56 T-bird, and '53 Corvette. However, the Cadillac was the first and grandest release. The brightly enameled stamped-sheet-metal car bodies bolted to hefty sheet-metal chassis. While the interior bothers that element of hard-core toy collectors who snub anything plastic, it was an injection-molded plastic tub that was cleanly finished, though perhaps a bit generic in detail. Its depth precluded the location of the silky-smooth friction/flywheel motor on the rear axle where it rightfully belonged. As a result, the FIFTIES mini-Cad became a front-wheel driver by default! This was a minor gripe, but a strange anachronism, since the first production FWD Cadillac was the 1967 Eldorado. While one can probably fault proportions, the high-quality chromed die-cast bumpers, whitewall tires, tiny fender scripts, and plastic taillight and headlight lens were strikingly beautiful. This was a quality friction-powered toy really too good to ever see serious "play" on the living room rug by little Cadillac buffs. This collectible toy belonged on the mantle.

Inside each box was a mock vehicle-registration card, a nice touch since each FIFTIES Cadillac had a unique serial number stamped on the rear license plate. Future

1950 coupe modified to replicate Briggs Cunningham's #3 Le Mans coupe, FIFTIES pressed steel.

1950 Cadillac at Mobil gas station, in pressed steel from unknown Japanese manufacturer; note the operating lift!

Ceramic bank (manufacturer unknown), in the form of a Series 62 coupe

1950 "Fix-It" plastic convertible, from Ideal. Included jack, spare tire, tools, and gas can for hours of play value. The shipping box became a garage.

Some of the many color variations of Praline's plastic 1950 coupe — red, cream, black, metallic blue, chestnut, and gray — pulled up to a Dairy Queen promotional bank, in plastic by unknown manufacturer

1950 convertibles by Praline

toy experts will probably unravel the significance of the inscrutable numbering system employed, but collectors have already separated these tin Cadillacs into early and later series. The early series lacked the "Cadillac" front fender script and the red dot in the middle of the hubcap; both features were present on the later series.

An interesting sidelight to the tin FIFTIES Cadillac story is the Chinese "Luxe Car #330 Type 1950." When the supply of new FIFTIES Cadillacs disappeared suddenly, the Chinese stepped in with a crude copy. Priced less than the Japanese original, the Luxe version is available in black or pink Series 62 coupe only.

Further, an unknown Taiwan manufacturer made an 11" ceramic 1950 coupe in hollow bank form. It also appears to be an unabashed copy of the tin FIFTIES or Luxe Cadillac. Copyright and patent laws are vague in the Far East.

Berkeley Models (USA) offered a 1⁄24-scale balsa wood kit of the Cadillac-powered Allard J-2 during the early 1950s. Since the kit offered little more than a roughly shaped wood block, rubber tires, and a waxed paper bag full of crudely cast metal trim, this was a difficult model to build. This kit probably scared away most model builders who lacked healthy imaginations.

During the 1970s Grand Prix Models of England offered a "white" metal kit of the venerable Cadillac-Allard J-2X sports racer. Crude and heavily encrusted with molding flash, this 1⁄43-scale model exemplified the problems with fine detail in early "white" metal kits. Nonetheless, it is a must in a Cadillac collection.

A popular toy during the early 1950s was an Ideal Toy Corporation (USA) Series 62 "Fix-it" convertible. Ideal intended its mini-Cadillac for the junior mechanic and included working jack, jerry can, screwdriver, hammer, wheel wrench, and tire iron to go in the cavernous opening trunk. In addition, the gas tank, radiator, oil sump, and battery all have removable caps and can be filled with liquids for hours of play value. In most respects, this 13" model is a reasonably faithful replica of a 1950 Cadillac. However, under the opening hood is a generic, in-line, four-cylinder engine.

For many years Frenchman Rene Dauffure created an extensive line of handmade wooden models in 1⁄43-scale, under the "Manou" label from his workshop not far from the Le Mans auto racing circuit. His version of the 1950 Cunningham Le Mans "Petit Petaud" is probably more auto folk art than scale model, but it is a prized addition to any collection (it is pictured in the Introduction to this book). Sadly, Dauffure's work is history, for he suffered serious health problems some years ago that ended model production — a loss for all miniature auto collectors.

John Day Models of England produced a line of simple "white" metal kits during the 1970s that included an accurate model of the rebodied Cunningham Le Mans Cadillac, "Le Monstre." Just like the real car, the model is large despite its diminutive 1⁄43 scale. The only other manufacturer to reproduce this landmark machine in miniature was Provence Moulage of France. Its 1⁄43-scale resin kit is current, simple, and accurate with photo-etched details that the John Day model lacks.

A recent partnership in manufacturing and distribution between Praline (Germany) and Revell (USA) has produced a line of tiny HO-scale 1950 Cadillacs for the model railroad trade. Available in convertible (top-up or top-down) and coupe bodies, these tiny Cadillacs come in distinct deluxe and regular series. The deluxe series sports plated bumpers and hubcaps while the regular series has silver painted trim. Deluxe versions also have a spare tire stuck to the trunk lid to incorrectly simulate a continental kit. All of the Praline/Revell Cadillacs are carefully silkscreened with side trim and deck emblems and offer great value for only a few dollars.

Premier's plastic kit for the 1950 Cadillac-powered Allard J-2X roadster

One of Solido's wind-up die-casts: 1950 sedan

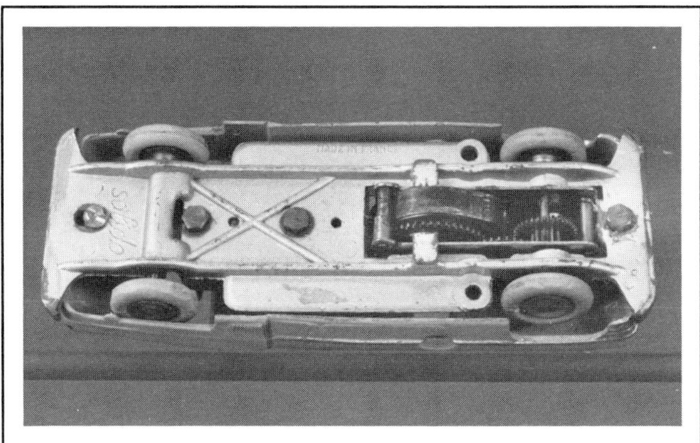

Detail of chassis in Solido die-cast 1950 sedan

Three die-casts from Vitesse: 1950 coupe, fire chief's car, and a circus car

Premier (USA) was one of the first plastic-kitmakers in the 1950s, and it made a toylike 1⁄24-scale Cadillac-Allard J-2X. Plated trim brightens an otherwise elementary model. Lack of fine detail keeps collector prices down on most Premier models.

During the 1950s Solido of France made a series of wind-up 1⁄43-scale die-cast models with interchangeable bodies. One of these bodies was a 1950-style Cadillac sedan with a large circular hole cut in the side for the key to the clockwork motor. This was a poorly detailed model but an interesting toy car for its construction and keywind power.

Structo (USA) is well known for its many toy truck models of the 1950s. One car-carrier toted a set of four 6" metal 1950 Series 61 coupes of very basic detail. These cars show up with some regularity at toy shows and flea markets, often without the car-carrier truck.

Vitesse of Portugal currently makes a nicely detailed 1950 Series 62 coupe that will please collectors who cannot bring themselves to pay the price for a French Elegance model. Offered in many colors, the Vitesse model comes with tiny chromed plastic door handles and mirrors that have to be installed by the collector. In addition, hood and rear deck emblems are decals. Special variations include a San Francisco fire chief's car, a "Circus Knie" loudspeaker car, and a Cunningham Le Mans coupe. Proportions are off, but the price is right. Vitesse recently released a top-up version of a 1950 convertible (reworked from the Series 62 coupe mold) as a companion piece. Unfortunately, when the coupe roof was removed, the convertible windshield that Vitesse designers substituted was an incorrect wraparound affair taken from the Vitesse 1953 Eldorado mold.

Wyandotte (USA) made a 1⁄24-scale Series 61 coupe that is often mistaken for some kind of promotional model. It is a simple toy with plastic body, no interior, separate plastic bumpers (some plated, some not), and a metal chassis with a flywheel motor. One obvious inaccuracy is

Note the incorrect windshield on the 1950 raised-top convertible die-cast by Vitesse, ***on the left*** *(the wraparound windshield did not appear on the real car until the debut of the 1953 Eldorado);* ***to the right****, three color variations of the coupe, again by Vitesse.*

the post that divides the windshield. The Wyandotte Caddy was available again in the early 1960s with a correct wraparound windshield. Nonetheless, it is a nice toy with great eye appeal, for it captures the lines of the car very well. Wyandotte also made a metal and plastic car-carrier set that toted a cargo of plastic 1⁄32-scale 1950 coupes that had obviously been pantographed into smaller scale from the 1⁄24-scale car.

1950

Alskog Design (Sweden): coupe, 5¼", vinyl toy with big tires; current; common. **$2 – 6**

AMR (France) 308: Series 61 convertible, 1⁄43, "white" metal kit, unpainted; obsolete; very rare. **$50 – 90**

AMR (France): Cunningham Series 61 Le Mans coupe, 1⁄43, "white" metal; obsolete; very rare. Conversion of AMR convertible. **$50 – 90**

Arcor Safe-Play Toys (USA): Series 62 sedan, 1⁄32, red-painted rubber; obsolete; rare. **$35 – 65**

Beetland (China): Coupe de Ville, 7¾", tin pencilbox; obsolete; less common. **$3 – 12**

Berkeley (USA): Allard J-2 roadster, 1⁄25, wood kit, unpainted; obsolete; rare. **$15 – 35**

Elegance (France) 107: Fleetwood seven-passenger sedan, 1⁄43, resin; current; rare. Low production, high price. **$125 – 300**

Elegance (France) 108: Series 75 Derham seven-passenger, 1⁄43, resin; black; current; rare. Low production, high price. **$200 – 475**

Elegance (France) 109: Series 62 two-door coupe, 1⁄43, resin; current; rare. Low production, high price. **$125 – 300**

Friction-powered plastic model of 1950 coupe by Wyandotte, appropriately enough in front of a Cadillac billboard (manufacturer unknown)

Elegance (France) 111: Series 60 Special four-door sedan, 1⁄43, resin; current; rare. Low production, high price. **$125 – 300**

Elegance (France) 113: Series 62 four-door sedan, 1⁄43, resin; current; rare. Low production, high price. **$150 – 300**

Elegance (France) 115: Series 86 NYC fire ambulance, 1⁄43, resin; red; current; rare. Low production, high price. **$200 – 300**

Elegance (France) 115b: Series 86 ambulance, 1⁄43, resin; white; current; rare. **$200 – 300**

Elegance (France) 124: Series 86 funeral hearse, 1⁄43, resin; current; rare. Low production, high price. **$200 – 300**

Elegance (France) 125: Series 86 funeral service car, 1⁄43, resin; current; rare. Low production, high price. **$200 – 300**

Elegance (France) 135: Series 75 Derham four-door limousine, 1⁄43, resin; current; rare. Low production, high price. **$200 – 300**

FIFTIES (Japan): Series 62 convertible, 11", "tin"; obsolete; less common. Friction. **$25 – 50**

FIFTIES (Japan): Series 62 coupe, 11", "tin"; obsolete; less common. Friction. **$20 – 50**

Grand Prix Models (GB): Cad-Allard open sportster, 1⁄43, "white" metal kit, unpainted; less common. **$20 – 50**

Ideal (USA): convertible, 13", plastic; rare — when complete. Many fix-it toy accessories. **$25 – 125**

John Day Models (GB): Le Monstre Cunningham racer, 1⁄43, "white" metal kit; white/blue; obsolete; rare. **$65 – 100**

Luxe Car (China) M 330: Series 62 coupe; "tin"; pink or black; current; common. Copy of FIFTIES version. **$10 – 25**

Praline/Revell (Germany) 83405: coupe, HO, plastic; current; common. Comes with plated or painted bumpers. **$2 – 6**

Praline/Revell (Germany) 83406: Eldorado convertible, HO, plastic; current; common. Some with continental kit; convertible with up or down top. **$2 – 6**

Premier (USA): Cad-Allard open sportster, 1/24, plastic kit; obsolete; rare. **$15 – 35**

Provence Moulage (France): Le Monstre Cunningham racer, 1/43, resin kit, unpainted; obsolete; less common. **$20 – 35**

RD Manou (France) 91: Series 61 coupe Cunningham racer, 1/43, wood and celluloid, handmade; white or blue; obsolete; rarest. **$75 – 150**

Solido (France): sedan, 1/43, die-cast; obsolete; rare. Keywind motor. **$75 – 125**

Structo (USA): Series 62 hardtop, 6", die-cast; obsolete; less common. From large auto-transport truck set. **$5 – 17**

Unknown (Taiwan): Series 62 hardtop, 11", ceramic; obsolete; less common. Appears to be a rip-off bank copy of tin FIFTIES Cad. **$5 – 20**

Vitesse (Portugal) 281: Series 62 convertible (top-up), 1/43, die-cast; current; common. Incorrect wraparound windshield from Vitesse 1953 Eldorado. **$10 – 25**

Vitesse (Portugal) 282: Series 62 coupe, 1/43, die-cast; current; common. **$10 – 25**

Vitesse (Portugal) 283: Cunningham Le Mans racer, 1/43, die-cast; current; common. The real car was actually a Series 61 coupe — not Series 62 as labeled here. **$10 – 25**

Vitesse (Portugal) 284: Series 62 coupe/red San Francisco fire chief's car, 1/43, die-cast; current; common. **$10 – 25**

Vitesse (Portugal) 285: Series 62 convertible (top-down), 1/43, die-cast; current; common. Correct windshield, unlike top-up version. **$10 – 25**

Vitesse (Portugal) 287: Series 62 coupe/"Circus Knie" car, 1/43; die-cast; red; current; common. **$10 – 25**

Wyandotte (USA): Series 62 coupe, 5½", plastic; obsolete; less common. No interior, snap-in wheels; used on transporter set. **$5 – 12**

Wyandotte (USA): Coupe de Ville, 1/24, plastic; obsolete; rare. Tin chassis with friction drive, no interior. **$30 – 60**

1951–1953

The Automobile

The Korean War diverted crucial materials to war production, and thus American automakers found the government limiting auto production. Despite these hardships, Cadillac had its greatest sales year to date in 1951. In addition, tank production kept Cadillac assembly lines humming. By 1952 the situation in Korea had worsened, and it was feared that auto production would once again be halted altogether in favor of war production. A steel strike also crippled heavy industries until President Harry S. Truman stepped in to seize control of the mills.

Cadillac management made a crucial production decision to discontinue the lower-priced Series 61 for 1952. From then on Cadillac abandoned the mid-priced field and concentrated its efforts on the higher-priced luxury-car market. By contrast, Packard had abandoned the luxury-car field, where it had once established its preeminence, to concentrate on medium-priced cars that eventually cost Packard much of the prestige of its name — and ultimately its future.

Styling changes were minimal to 1953, for Cadillac had back orders to fill and hence little reason for major change. Grille trim was tastefully retroweled in 1952, and twin "Dagmar" grille bullets were added for 1953 (Dagmar was the name of a physically well-endowed female TV personality of the early 1950s, and the anatomical metaphor was not lost on GM stylists). In addition, the 1953 Cadillacs received one-piece rear windows.

Cadillac stylists were not asleep during these years. The traveling GM Motorama showcased dream cars that forecast GM cars yet to come and gauged public response to bold new styling themes before they were committed to production. The Eldorado started as the specially trimmed Series 62 convertible with wraparound windshield, hard boot, and plush interior introduced at the 1952 Motorama extravaganza. When the public responded positively, Cadillac tooled up for a small, token 1953 production run. This helped establish Cadillac as the continuing style leader when Cadillac styling changes were otherwise slow to come. Showmanship such as this brought customers into showrooms even if few of the mostly handbuilt Eldorados were actually made.

Paralleling the development of special two-seat sports cars by her sister GM divisions, Cadillac also built a short-wheelbase fiberglass sportster dubbed the Le Mans (a name that capitalized on the marque's 1950 success at the classic French endurance race). The rakish Le Mans dream car forecast the front-end styling for the upcoming 1954 line. Although the Le Mans was not a serious effort at a sporting production vehicle, several copies were made. One drivable example survives to this day in fine condition in the showroom of Maryland Cadillac dealer Jim Coleman.

Another dream car was the Orleans, a luxurious four-door hardtop that first displayed a popular styling motif that spread to other GM lines. The elimination of the heavy center post between front and rear doors gave the Orleans (and subsequent large GM cars) a light airy appearance that the public loved. Once again, the competition was forced into catch-up mode.

1951–1953 in Miniature

In the late 1980s French modelmaker Elegance created a lovely 1⁄43-scale 1951 Series 62 convertible that made a fine companion piece to the 1950 line of Elegance Cadillacs. In addition, a custom-bodied Coachcraft station wagon and the Series 86 six-door King Ibn Seoud "haremmobile" was offered. Again, Elegance models sell for several hundreds of dollars and are difficult to find.

American toymaker Ertl makes a die-cast 1⁄43-scale 1952 Series 62 sedan in pink and white with silver-painted side trim and window surrounds as well as in a light blue and white version. Retailing for less than ten dollars, the Ertl model is a bargain. Ertl also makes an all-black version of the same serial number available in a special American-car gift set sold only through the Toys "R" Us chain stores. Another variation — one that might seem appropriate only in a circus parade — is a yellow and red version with Shop-Rite foodstore graphics on the doors and trunk.

Sun Models of England took the Ertl 1⁄43-scale die-cast 1952 Cadillac, discarded the metal body, and substituted its own resin body to convert the sedan into a Series 75 limousine. The model came painted and factory assembled, using Ertl wheels, bumpers, and trim pieces. Although not the fine quality of the French Elegance limo, the Sun Models version cost considerably less!

Banthrico of Chicago (Bank Thrift Company) produced a full line of static models and car banks slush molded in bright pot metal in (approximately) 1⁄25 scale. These model cars featured black rubber tires mounted on metal hubs and axles. Most sported metal baseplates with coin slots and key-locking trap doors. These hefty toy banks readily fit a child's hand. Bumpers, trim, and windows were masked before the body was spray painted so they would show up silver when the masks were removed. Banthrico's aggressive marketing sold thousands of these models to car dealers, savings and loans, and banks by silkscreening customized advertising messages on the roofs. The Banthrico 1952 1⁄25-scale Series 62 sedan is a highly desirable model/bank, even though its pudgy proportions are less than accurate. Such promotional items of yesterday are the collectibles of today and tomorrow.

Cottage-industry TKM Models offered 1⁄25-scale resin kits of the 1952 Series 62 convertible and sedan as well as a 1953 Series 60 Special and the 1953 Eldorado convertible. These are not simple kits to make, for they require much handwork, but they have few parts and are easy to paint.

Miller Memorabilia also offered a resin 1952 Series 62 four-door sedan similar to the Banthrico.

Japanese toymakers of the late 1940s and early 1950s are well known among serious toy collectors for the pressed-steel toy cars that became the mainstay of an export industry that rose from the ashes of World War II devastation. Early examples were often actually pressed and pounded out of leftover sheet-metal cans and containers (thus the "tin" nickname) when resources were scarce. Japanese toymakers achieved great fidelity and charm in their work, and certain "tin" cars bring hundreds and even thousands of dollars today from collectors. Marusan of Japan made a beautiful 11" 1951 Series 60 Special in a variety of colors. Some of these toys even sported battery-powered electric lights and/or friction motors. Collectors' prices on the Marusan Cadillacs have climbed quickly during the 1980s, and mint-boxed examples are very desirable and expensive.

Alps (Japan) made an 11½" tin 1952 Series 62 convertible that is also a highly desirable toy. Alps' tin Cadillacs are often confused with the Marusan toys, but their differences are obvious when placed side by side with the Marusans. The Alps Cadillacs were larger and had open cast grillework and bumper-mounted number plates.

A similar (but less detailed) 13" 1952 convertible was made by Japanese toymaker Nomura. The Nomura "Electricmobile" convertible had battery-powered lights

Heavy traffic at the Plasticville Turnpike Interchange: various 1952 four-door sedans, die-cast by Ertl

and was an odd four-door configuration that would lead one to believe that it was cut down from a sedan model toy. Taillights were more Chrysler-like than Cadillac-like, and the front fender "Cadillac" script was omitted.

Auburn Rubber (USA) made a 5½" squeezably soft 1953 Le Mans two-seat Motorama show car (#0176 on its license plate). Front-end styling was unmistakably Cadillac, but Auburn's designers got carried away with extra geegaws, such as a continental kit and brougham taillights. A large woman driver and an ugly dog were molded into the interior. This was a sporty Cadillac toy that was indestructible. A fascinating Auburn companion piece was a 5½" fantasy Motorama show car that combined the Le Mans front-end design with the Motorama Corvette Waldorf ("Nomad") station wagon roof line. Molded in the same soft vinyl as the Le Mans, #0178 was on the rear number plate. Perhaps GM's styling department should have recruited the toymaker's design team, for a Cadillac sport wagon might have started a whole new specialty car market! Auburn also made a smaller 4¾" Le Mans that was similar to the four-headlight 1959 restyling of a real 1953 Le Mans show car that exists to this day at Dixon Cadillac in Hollywood. Hood and rear deck were painted silver, a well-fed couple was molded into the driver and passenger seats, and #504 was molded into the rear number plate. Fender-mounted trumpet horns and streamlined headrests were imaginative Auburn additions. Auburn Rubber toy Cadillacs reflected the exuberance and outrageously optimistic styling cliches of the early 1950s. These vinyl toys were made in large quantity for many years. Later versions were in vinyl rather than hard rubber.

This 1952 four-door sedan serves as a bank, slush-cast pot metal by Banthrico.

Manoil (USA) was also inspired by the 1959 restyle of the 1953 Le Mans and made an inexpensive 5¾" die-cast toy that was loosely based upon this sporty two-seater. People often mistake this toy for a Tootsietoy.

Midgetoy of Rockford, Illinois, made a die-cast 3½" stylized version of the Le Mans show car that was a dime-store toy of the 1950s. Many of these show up at toy train shows as remnants of Christmas garden displays. Lack of detail keeps prices low.

Goodee Products (of New Brunswick, New Jersey) made a die-cast 3" 1953 Eldorado convertible. This was a crude 1950s dime store toy that is often confused with the similarly sized Tootsietoys that were the poor man's Matchbox cars. Prices are still low for these toys.

In 1990 Danbury Mint released a highly detailed 1⁄16-scale metal and plastic model of the 1953 Eldorado.

The nonauthentic four-door configuration probably indicates that this pressed-steel convertible was cut down from a sedan die; it is believed to be by Nomura (Ferd Zegel Collection).

Influenced by the 1952 Motorama show car: ***Top:*** *Nomad-style station wagon dream car and Le Mans show car by Auburn Rubber.* ***Bottom:*** *Le Mans show car by Auburn* ***(left)*** *and a die-cast by Manoil* ***(right).***

Doors, hood, and trunk open on this sleek white 14" convertible to reveal extraordinary detailing. Even the seats are upholstered in red leather. The hard parade boot for the top-down version is included along with a molded-plastic raised top that snaps into place. Danbury Mint craftsmen really did their homework on this museum-quality Eldo. Available by mail order, this beautiful model sells for $200. Perhaps those collectors who have trouble rationalizing such a cash outlay for a model might take solace in the fact that, pound for pound, this is a hefty bargain that requires the use of two strong hands to pick it up and move it!

In the 1950s English toymaker Dinky Toy die-cast a 1/48-scale 1953 Eldorado convertible that came painted pinkish or yellow. A tiny scale driver watched the road from behind the stylish plastic wraparound windshield. However, the car body seemed a bit on the long side. The Eldo remained in the Dinky catalog for many years as a popular model, but current prices for a mint-boxed Dinky Cadillac are getting away from the casual collector's reach.

Franklin Mint produced a 1953 Eldorado convertible that, at first glance, (see page 71) seems to be a smaller 1/24-scale copy of the Danbury Mint model. Look again. While the mail-order Franklin Mint model is pleasing and less expensive, it also lost something in the translation to smaller scale — accuracy. The hood and cowling are completely inaccurate, probably an engineering concession to make the hood hinges work properly. It is a nice model, but it is not up to the quality of other Franklin 1/24-scale productions.

Tootsietoy (USA) currently sells a Chinese-made 5" die-cast metal 1953 Eldorado convertible in its inexpensive "Hard Body" series of special-interest American cars. Trimmed in black and chrome-plated plastic, it is sold individually blister-packed or in boxed gift sets with other cars. These are tough play toys. The mag-style wheels and wide racing tires (common to all numbers in the series) are more appropriate for a Ferrari Testa Rossa, and there is an odd strip of chrome mylar tape for decoration just behind each front wheel cutout. Perhaps the silver

***Top:** 1953 Eldorado pencil erasers from Russ. **Bottom:** Midgetoy fantasy dream car; '53 Eldorado convertible, a Goodee die-cast; '53 Motorama Le Mans show car, die-cast by Midgetoy.*

tape was an attempt to mimic the chrome side grilles of the Cadillac El Camino and La Espada Motorama show cars? With the substitution of more realistic wheels and the removal of the tape side trim, this is a reasonable miniature with poor build quality at an inexpensive price. This toy cries out for detailing from a patient hand.

Portuguese toymaker Vitesse makes an inexpensive die-cast 1/43-scale 1953 Eldorado convertible (top-down, #280/top-up, #281.) Notable variations include a white Eldorado convertible with bumper-mounted Presidential flags and figures of President Dwight D. Eisenhower with his driver as well as a pink version with a Marilyn Monroe-like figure perched on the front fender. The most glaring inaccuracy is the use of Sabre-style wheels from a newer Eldorado when wire wheels would be correct.

At first glance a current Chinese die-cast 1953 Eldorado toy would seem to be a direct copy of the Vitesse model. However, it is slightly larger than 1/43-scale and lacks the correct wraparound windshield. The plastic chassis has a pull-back-and-release spring motor that will propel the car across the floor. Details are crude, deck emblems are missing, doors hinge open, and no manufacturer name or logo is indicated. "NO. 8802" is molded on the plastic underside of both top-up and top-down versions. Plated bumpers and a low price make this a bargain toy.

In the spirit of 1950s nostalgia, SDD produced a wonderfully tacky ceramic salt-and-pepper set that replicates a pink 1/43-scale 1953 Eldorado convertible and a Googie-style drive-in hot dog stand. The hot dog stand pepper shaker is turquoise and white with a glossy black roof. The service windows and door detail are decals, and the twin shaker holes are in the middle of the rakishly angled roof. The shaker hole for the Eldorado salt shaker is at the front of the hood where the hood ornament would go, and "SDD c 1989 #442" is scribed into the otherwise featureless chassis. What a fun way to add color to a fast food lunch!

The last 1953 Eldorado model is not a model at all but a currently available 2" pencil eraser that comes in a variety of garish colors. Bizarre, but still Cadillac.

Danbury Mint's die-cast 1953 Eldorado convertible has working doors, hood, trunk, and steering; German train station backdrop.

Vitesse has brought out many color variations of its die-cast 1953 Eldorado convertible.

1951

Elegance (France) 118: Series 62 convertible, 1/43, resin; current; rare. Low production, high price. #118b is boxer Sugar Ray Robinson's pink convertible. **$150 – 300**

Elegance (France) 131: Coachcraft station wagon, 1/43, resin; current; rare. Low production, high price. **$150 – 300**

Marusan (Japan): Series 60 Special, 11", "tin"; obsolete; rarest. **$600 – 1200**

1952

Alps (Japan): convertible, 11½", "tin"; obsolete; rarest. **$600 – 1200**

Banthrico (USA): four-door sedan, 1/25, pot metal; obsolete; rare. Toy bank with silkscreened ad on roof. **$90 – 150**

1953 Eldorado convertible in Tootsietoy's Hard Body series

The Eldorado convertible of 1953, die-cast by Dinky Toy

President Dwight D. Eisenhower's inaugural parade car from Vitesse; note the "D.C. 1" license plate on the 1953 Eldorado.

These die-cast 1953 Eldorado convertibles are powered by pull-back/spring-forward motors. Note incorrect windshield; Eldorados all sported the revolutionary wraparound windshield in 1953. The Frosty Bar is by Plasticville, the plastic figures by Lifelike.

1953 Eldorado convertible and hot dog stand salt-and-pepper set in ceramic by SDD

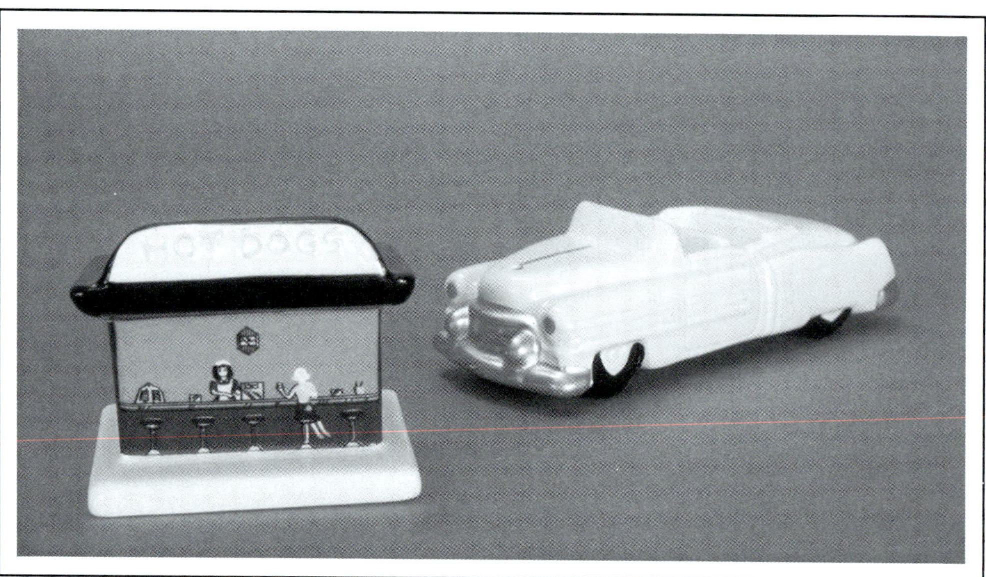

Franklin Mint's Eldorado convertible. It is more accurate than the Danbury Mint model on page 67.

Elegance (France) 117: Series 86 six-door King Ibn Seoud, 1/43, resin; current; rare. Low production, high price. **$150 – 300**

Ertl (USA): four-door sedan, 1/43, die-cast; standard pink/white or light blue/white; current; common. **$3 – 10**

Ertl (USA): four-door sedan, 1/43, die-cast; solid black gift set version; current; less common. **$5 – 15**

Ertl (USA): four-door sedan, 1/43, die-cast; yellow/red with "Shop-Rite" graphics; obsolete; less common. **$5 – 15**

Sun (GB) 123: Series 75 limousine, 1/43, resin; current; less common. Conversion body using Ertl trim. **$30 – 65**

Toys Namura (Japan): four-door convertible, 13", "tin"; black; obsolete; rarest. **$400 – 800**

1953

Auburn Rubber (USA) 0176 (shown on license plate): Le Mans two-seat sportster (GM Motorama dream car), 5½", soft rubber; obsolete; less common. Crude, extra trim not on real show car. **$5 – 15**

Auburn Rubber (USA) 0178: Motorama station wagon dream car, 5¼", vinyl; obsolete; less common. Fictional cross between Le Mans and Waldorf Nomad station wagon show cars. **$5 – 15**

Danbury Mint (USA): Eldorado convertible, 1/16, metal/plastic/leather; white; current; common. By mail order. An extraordinary model! **$100 – 200 (new)**

Dinky (GB) 131: Eldorado convertible, 4½", die-cast; tan or yellow; obsolete; rare. Rapidly appreciating. **$50 – 150**

Franklin Mint (USA): Eldorado convertible, 1/24, metal/plastic; white; current; common. By mail order. **$35 – 125**

Goodee (USA): Eldorado convertible, 3", die-cast; obsolete; less common. Crude dime store toy. **$4 – 10**

Midgetoy (USA): Le Mans Motorama show car, 3½", die-cast; obsolete; less common. Crude toy interpretation. **$4 – 10**

Nomura (Japan): Le Mans show car, 10⅜"; tin; silver/red; obsolete; rarest. Has operating headlights. **$300 – 450**

Russ (Hong Kong): Eldorado convertible (top-up), 2", soft rubber pencil eraser; current; common. **$.25 – 1**

SDD (country of origin unknown) 442: Eldorado convertible as hot dog stand salt-and-pepper set; ceramic; obsolete; less common. **$6 – 12**

Tootsietoy (USA): Eldorado convertible, 5", die-cast/plastic; current; common. Hard Body series, made in China. **$1 – 5**

Unknown (China) 8802: Eldorado convertible (incorrect windshield; top-up and top-down versions available), 4¾", die-cast; current; common. Recoil motor. Possible pantographed copy of Vitesse model. **$1 – 3**

Vitesse (Portugal) 280: Eldorado convertible (top-down), 1⁄43, die-cast; current; common. **$12 – 25**

Vitesse (Portugal) 281: Eldorado convertible (top-up), 1⁄43, die-cast; current; common. **$12 – 25**

Vitesse (Portugal) 286: Eldorado convertible parade car (top-down) for President Eisenhower, 1⁄43, die-cast; white; obsolete; common. Presidential flags, figures of driver and President Eisenhower. **$12 – 25**

Vitesse (Portugal) 288: Eldorado convertible (top-down), 1⁄43, die-cast; pink; current; common. Marilyn Monroe version, with movie star perched on fender. **$12 – 25**

1954

The Automobile

The McCarthy years were uncertain years for Americans. Korean peace talks dragged, and Southeast Asia showed signs of more trouble to come. Auto sales were off, and carmakers started to realize that the sellers' market had suddenly become a buyers' market. Nevertheless, Cadillac was still backlogged with orders.

Although Harley Earl still kept a watchful eye over styling development as a vice president, William Mitchell officially became director of GM styling. Cadillac restyled its cars to be longer, lower, and wider. The wraparound windshield that had been an Eldorado exclusive only a year before was now standard on all lesser Cadillacs. Coupes were all hardtops. The Eldorado was shifted to a Series 62 body to reduce production costs and its price, and the 1954 Motorama overflowed with impressive Cadillac show cars.

The Park Avenue Motorama show car was a styling study "town car" with an attractive brushed-stainless-steel roof. If the Park Avenue wasn't enough, Motorama viewers were wowed by a pair of svelte short-wheelbase sportsters that borrowed heavily from aircraft lines and predicted 1958 front-end styling that included quad headlights. The open version, dubbed "La Espada," sported wind-cheating rear deck headrests. Such a dream car must have set convertible lovers' hearts pounding as they watched the fiberglass "Apollo Gold" beauty revolve

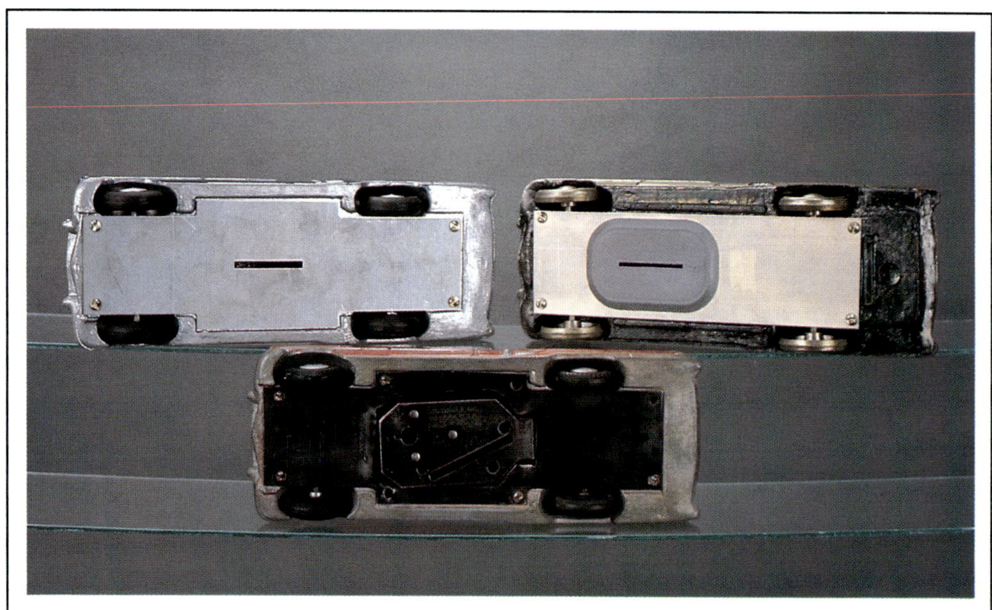

Chassis details of 1954 Cadillac 60 Special banks by Banthrico. ***Top:*** *1970s reproduction and 1980s reproduction, slush-cast pot metal.* ***Bottom:*** *Original chassis detail, with key lock.*

Top: *Cadillac 60 Special bank by Banthrico, 1970s reissue; note rubber wheels, as in original issue.* ***Bottom:*** *1980s reissue; crude brushed antique brass or pewter finish; note raised chassis to enable body to clear large, incorrectly sized metal wheels.*

Great American Dream Machines' interpretations of 1954 Motorama show cars: La Espada roadster and El Camino coupe

Battery-powered cable-remote control 1954 60 Special in pressed steel from Gama

on a lighted turntable in the futuristic Motorama display. La Espada's sister car, the El Camino, was a pearlescent silver hardtop version of the same basic design that previewed the 1957 Cadillac roof line to come. Flashy stainless grillework on the front fenders disguised air vents for engine and passenger compartments. Buck Rogers would have loved the Motorama show cars!

1954 in Miniature

The model-car industry of the 1950s was exciting to watch from the collector's standpoint. New plastics technology gave toy companies a medium that displaced more traditional materials. However, one well-established Chicago company, Banthrico, resisted this swing to plastics and continued to produce beautifully detailed static models and banks of current production cars in slush-molded pot metal. At the same time, several new companies started to make similarly sized models and banks from colorful plastics with separate chrome-plated bumpers and trim, friction motors, and two-tone paint jobs. These models were lighter than Banthricos and had clear windows and even interior detail in some cases. The Banthrico models were heavy banks and had opaque metal windows. The success of these new plastic "promotional" models made Banthrico's efforts pale in comparison, and a wise management realized that its future was in other more profitable product lines. Understandable business logic, but a loss for collectors. Before Banthrico finally quit producing contemporary production vehicles in 1956, it gave Cadillac collectors several fine Cadillac models.

In 1954 Banthrico made a Series 60 Special with black rubber tires on metal hubs. The slush-cast body was attached to a sheet-steel baseplate with a key-locked trap door in the chassis with a coin slot. The most desirable examples still have silkscreened advertising on the roof and original paint, although their relative rarity makes all but the most dented or playworn very desirable.

There is a later chapter to the Banthrico story, for in the 1970s Banthrico's management rediscovered its old dies and made a limited-production run of 1954 Cadillacs that were sold unpainted and with a baseplate that had no locking trap door. A good repaint might otherwise fool a collector, but the lack of the trap-door lock is a dead

This 1954 Eldorado convertible, die-cast by Mini Marque, is a beauty; note fine photo-etched details.

giveaway for a reproduction. These models, even though made in smaller numbers than the original, are worth about a quarter of that of an original.

To further confuse the potential Banthrico collector, Banthrico recast and re-released the 1954 Cadillac still again in the 1980s with horrible oversized metal tires and unappealing choices of brushed pewter or antique brass finish. Again these models omitted the key lock in the baseplate. Sloppy finishing and heavy grinding away of surface detail make these last issues worth only a few dollars. Banks and savings and loans ordered these new issues with silkscreened advertising, but the pewter and brass finishes are not especially attractive. What a sad fate for this otherwise nice model.

Galoob (China) made three Micromachines of 1954 Cadillacs — tiny, free-rolling, cartoonish versions that were included in gift sets of American cars. The Coupe de Ville and convertible are each only about 1½" long. The 2" customized Series 75 limo sports a black convertible (!) roof.

There are no models of the lovely Park Avenue Motorama dream car, but Great American Dream Machines (USA) offers beautifully factory-finished 1/43-scale models of the flashy El Camino sport coupe and its sister ship, the swoopy open La Espada, both die-cast by England's SMTS. GADM specializes in making high-quality models of factory dream cars, and the El Camino and La Espada were welcomed releases in a series that includes the exotic Le Sabre, the sporty Waldorf Nomad, and the dashing Buick Y-Job. Although expensive, these are fine miniatures that are current offerings.

Gama of Germany modified and updated the 1950 Marusan tin Cadillac dies to reflect 1954 specifications. Although the body still was the 1950-1953 shell, the grillework and wraparound windshield and rectangular vent windows reflected 1954 Series 60 Special styling cues. These motorized models had a remote-control and battery pack with a trailing cable that allowed the toy to be steered and driven forward or reverse. One has to remember that these 1950s toys were made long before microchip technology enabled toymakers to create inexpensive radio-controlled toys. So successful was this toy that Joustra of France produced it in turn after Gama. These are gems.

Talented Virginia modeler Sam Miller was dissatisfied with the model companies' standard offerings and created a whole cottage-industry line of resin kits of American cars under the Miller Memorabilia banner. His offerings spanned the breadth of the industry, but he offered several 1954 1/25-scale Cadillac models.

These kits did not include plated parts or fancy packaging, and they were individually handcast to order. Included were models of a Series 60 Special, a Series 62 convertible, a Fleetwood 75 limousine, and a Coupe de Ville. Cottage industries such as Miller Memorabilia offered items not otherwise offered in scale, and such models eventually attain a kind of automotive folk art status.

Mini Marque of England recently released a factory-finished die-cast 1/43-scale Eldorado with superb car photo-etched details. This is an expensive museum-quality replica produced in a variety of colors in top-up and top-down versions. This is one of the best 1⁄43-scale Cadillacs made, and the only 1954 Eldorado model offered in any scale.

Tootsietoy made a die-cast 5⅝" Series 62 sedan that was a lightly detailed contemporary toy. There was no interior, but some examples had a lithographed tin chassis. Most came painted two-tone with airbrushed silver bumper trim. Since Tootsietoy made many of these, they are not exceptionally hard to find. However, finding nonplayworn examples may be difficult.

1954

Banthrico (USA): Series 60 Special, 8¼", pot metal; obsolete; very rare. Original issue; advertising silkscreened on roof; rubber tires. **$90 – 200**

Banthrico (USA): Series 60 Special, 8¼", pot metal, unpainted; obsolete; rare. 1970s reissue bank; rubber tires, nonlocking baseplate. **$25 – 50**

Banthrico (USA): Series 60 Special, 8¼", pot metal; current; common. 1980s reissue bank; inferior metal tires and nonlocking baseplate. **$6 – 15**

Galoob (China): convertible, 1¼", plastic; light blue; current; common. Micromachine. **$.25 – 1**

Galoob (China): Coupe de Ville, 1¼", plastic; silver/white; current; common. Micromachine. **$.25 – 1**

Galoob (China): Customized Series 75 limousine, 1¾", plastic; red/black; current; common. Micromachine. **$.25 – 1**

Great American Dream Machines (USA) 5: La Espada roadster, 1⁄43; die-cast; metallic yellow; current; less common. Motorama dream car. **$100 – 160**

Great American Dream Machines (USA) 7: El Camino coupe, 1⁄43, die-cast; metallic silver; current; less common. Motorama dream car. **$100 – 160**

*Tootsietoy's large die-cast 1954 Series 62 sedan with **(left to right)** Galoob Micromachine plastic convertible, custom limousine, and Coupe de Ville*

Joustra (France)/Gama(Germany): Series 60 Special, 12", "tin"; obsolete; rarest. Electric motor; body originally from Marusan dies. **$600 – 1200**

Miller Memorabilia (USA) 5B: Series 62 convertible, 1⁄25, resin kit, unpainted; obsolete; less common. **$20 – 35**

Miller Memorabilia (USA) 5C: Fleetwood 75 limousine, 1⁄25, resin kit, unpainted; obsolete; less common. **$20 – 35**

Miller Memorabilia (USA) 5D: Coupe de Ville, 1⁄25, resin kit, unpainted; obsolete; less common. **$20 – 35**

Mini Marque (GB) 43: Eldorado convertible (top-up, top-down), 1⁄43, die-cast/plastic; current; less common. Handbuilt. **$100 – 225**

Stanley Ceramic Works (England): Series 60 Special cookie jar, 15"; green; obsolete; rare. China cookie jar with lift-off roof for cookie storage. **$50 – 125**

Tootsietoy (USA) 345: Series 62 sedan, 5⅝", die-cast; blue chassis/gray top or cream/red; obsolete; less common. Trailer hitch molded to rear bumper. **$12 – 40**

1955

The Automobile

Cadillac entered the second year of its three-year style cycle with orders still backlogged. Increases in horsepower made the 1955 model one of the quickest accelerating production cars. Styling changes on the bread-and-butter line were minor, but the Eldorado received the razor tail fins pioneered on the El Camino and La Espada show cars only a year before. Taillights and backup lights rode in tiny dummy jet nozzles at the base of each fin. In addition, the beautifully cast "Sabre-spoke" wheels first seen on the Le Mans Motorama car were introduced on the Eldorado.

The public's acceptance of the lovely Park Avenue from the 1954 Motorama inspired Harley Earl's dream car styling teams to produce one of the most striking project cars of all time for the 1955 Motorama line-up — the breathtaking Eldorado Brougham. It accurately predicted most features used on the production Brougham that would appear in March of 1957. Cadillac knew that such a knockout automobile would be necessary to counter Ford's upcoming Continental Mark II luxury specialty car. That battle would prove costly and bloody for both GM and Ford.

1955 in Miniature

Banthrico of Chicago face-lifted its 1⁄25-scale pot-metal 1954 Series 60 Special bank to reflect styling changes, but the 1955 issue was never again recast and reissued as was the 1954 version. Collectors will have to scramble to find the 1955 Banthrico Cadillac.

Model collectors are smart to watch model-railroad hobbyists, for occasionally they add interesting automotive items to their stock of railroad accessories. In the 1980s an American firm called Alloy Forms made a series of "white" metal 1950s vehicles in popular HO scale. These tiny cars and trucks were available unpainted and unassembled, or painted and assembled. The tiny 1955 Series 60 Special in this line appears to be a pantographed copy of the Banthrico 1⁄25-scale car bank! Alloy Forms went out of business, but its products are still in the distribution channels of most hobby-shop suppliers, and all should still be easy to find.

Aluminum Model Toys (AMT) was one of the first companies to popularize 1⁄25-scale "promotional" models. AMT's first product was an aluminum 1948 Ford, but soon AMT embraced plastics technology and offered a wide selection of attractively colored, acetate-bodied models with celluloid windows and even detailed interiors. These models often had sheet-steel chassis with flywheel-type friction motors. Stores sold them or dealers gave them away as sales promotions (hence, the nickname "promo"). Unfortunately the shiny acetate plastic car bodies had a nasty tendency to warp and deform as they shrank, and few early AMT models have escaped the ravages of time. Values suffer as a result. AMT was the first and, for many years, the only manufacturer to offer a 1955 Coupe de Ville. The AMT 1955 Cadillac featured plated metal bumpers and simulated front, side, and rear windows of vacuum-formed plastic. Deluxe models carried two-tone interior detail and plated hubcaps. Lesser (or economy) versions of the same model were available without interiors and with plain white plastic hubcaps. Another variation was equipped with a battery-powered electric drive motor and cable-operated remote control.

A novel thumb-operated air pump in the hand-held remote-control unit sent air down a flexible tube that paralleled the electric cable. This air pulse then inflated a tiny black rubber bladder hidden within the car model that would force the spring-loaded front axle to pivot and simulate steering action. Since the fragile rubber parts of the steering mechanism were prone to dry rot, remote-controlled examples of the AMT Cadillac often show up minus inoperative control units and even the electric motors. The odd center-pivot front axle is a dead giveaway of remote-control heritage.

Cottage-industry leader Miller Memorabilia offered a 1⁄25-scale resin kit similar to the Banthrico Series 60 Special. These were handcast kits made to order in small numbers.

American model-kit manufacturer Monogram issued beautiful 1⁄20-scale 1955 Series 62 convertible and Coupe de Ville kits. The main difference between the two kits was a top-down "boot" for the rear deck of the convertible and a white plastic hardtop that converted the handsome mini-Cad to a sport coupe. Although the model was heads above anything else offered at the time, it had two flaws. First, the windows were die-cut from sheet acetate; these were difficult to fit and not in keeping with the high quality of the rest of the model. Secondly, Monogram chose to mold the body in Tenite (a hard, glossy acetate plastic) that warped badly. The snap-on hardtop became useless as it curled with age. Bumpers were plated to simulate chrome, and the convertible version was usually molded in red or light blue, while the Coupe de Ville variation was usually molded in yellow. The most prized variation on this kit is the factory-made sample that was given to hobby dealers to tempt hobbyists into buying the plastic kit.

Motor City (USA) made a 1⁄43-scale die-cast Fleetwood Series 60 Special that seemed to be another pantograph of the Banthrico car bank. However, the Motor City model had separate bumpers, clear windows, and a full interior. Now out of production, this was a carefully finished model with fine detail and excellent paint. Available in burgundy, metallic gray, or white with a black roof, this die-cast is a desirable Cadillac model.

Premier models made a plastic 1955 Eldorado convertible and hardtop in (roughly) 1⁄25 scale. This was a primitive effort at kit design, although trim parts were plated to simulate chrome. Typical of the crude plastic models that replaced the clunky, hard-to-build wooden kits of the late 1940s, these early kits still left much to be desired. Lack of accurate detail keeps Premier kit prices down today unless they are mint, boxed, and unbuilt. Collectors value such primitive kits for their historical significance rather than their fidelity to detail.

Processed Plastics, an American toy company known for vinyl plastic toys, made a (roughly) 1⁄30-scale 1955 convertible with snap-in wheels and a clear plastic wraparound windshield.

Unfortunately, body and bumper trim were all molded in the same color. A companion-piece coupe was also available. Fun.

A not-to-be-repeated collaboration between rival model companies AMT and Revell produced a plastic 1⁄32-scale Eldorado convertible kit that was among the finest of its day. The body shell was formed from several panels of polystyrene plastic to be glued together by the modeler. The resulting model captured much of the car's elegance and dash. The tiny plastic figures of the handsome tuxedoed driver and his lovely high-heeled and fur-draped female companion (a charming bonus in each kit) now recall nostalgia for those happy Eisenhower years. The most desirable variation of this kit is the factory-assembled sample given to hobby dealers.

1955 Cadillac Fleetwoods. ***Back to front:*** *Banthrico's 1⁄25-scale slush-cast pot-metal bank, 1⁄43-scale die-cast by Motor City, presumed to be pantographed from the Banthrico bank; a HO-scale die-cast kit from Alloy Form, which is presumed to be pantographed from Motor City or Banthrico models.*

AMT 1955 Coupe de Ville, with original packing box that can be made into a garage

1955 Series 62 convertible, from Monogram's plastic kit, pulled up to gas pumps from unknown manufacturer

1955 Eldorado convertible; this Premier kit is one of the earliest 1/25-scale plastic model kits made.

Coming and going, the Eldorado Brougham Motorama show car, die-cast by Structo

Ronnie's Ceramic Company (USA) made a 1955 Coupe de Ville candy dish in two-tone pink china. Cartoonish and vaguely detailed, this novelty gift-shop item appeals to the current nostalgia for the 1950s.

Solido of France released a large 1/18-scale die-cast 1955 Eldorado in the spring of 1990. The top-down version is painted a very *non*-stock pink while the top-up version is a deep metallic turquoise. These are nice current offerings for the money with steerable front wheels, opening doors, and plated bumpers and trim. Deck emblems are "peel-and-stick" decals. One odd flaw is the lack of vent windows. Since this is a large model, such an omission stands out.

No doubt Solido will be true to past performance and create a number of color variations on the '55 Eldorado to please color collectors before ending production.

Structo (USA) made the only model of the 1955 Eldorado Brougham Motorama show car. Although detail was vague, and it lacked windows or interior, this die-cast metal 1/35-scale toy was made for rugged play as cargo on a basic 1950s metal car-transporter truck. Special plated versions that commemorated some company anniversary or milestone sported a special decal. These obsolete toys frequently are found without the transport truck at shows.

The last 1955 Cadillac models offered are current 1/43-scale models by the Swiss modelmaker Zaugg. The resin Coupe de Ville body is finished in glossy red with a white top, but the chassis, side trim, and bumpers are bright plated die-cast metal. While the Zaugg coupe is a highly detailed factory-assembled model, the biggest problem is with the roof line; the pattern maker forgot the rear package shelf. As a result, the rear window has an odd slant that does not do the rest of the car justice. The top-down convertible version of the same car eliminated the roof problem by default. Zaugg also offered the

1955 Series 62 convertible and '55 Coupe de Ville, both vinyl plastics from Processed Plastics

1955 Eldorado convertible, as represented by the plastic Revell/AMT kit

Coupe de candy dish: Ronnie's Ceramics 1955 Coupe de Ville

convertible as an unbuilt kit. One easy way to tell if a Zaugg model is factory assembled or finished from the less expensive kit is to check the seats. The factory-assembled convertibles have the ribbed upholstery pattern simulated by decals. The kit's seats are undecaled. The factory-assembled version also has tiny decaled chrome hashmarks above the rear bumper. The kit version incorrectly deletes these. Zaugg model prices reflect their intensive handwork and rarity, and the factory-assembled cars should cost more.

1955

Alloy Forms (USA): Series 60 Special four-door, 1/87, "white" metal kit, unpainted; obsolete; less common. Pantograph of Banthrico. **$3 – 10**

AMT (USA): Coupe de Ville, 1/25, plastic/friction drive promo model; obsolete; less common. **$50 – 100**

Banthrico (USA): Series 60 Special four-door, 1/25, pot metal bank, original issue; obsolete; very rare. **$90 – 200**

Miller Memorabilia (USA) 115: Fleetwood 60 four-door, 1/25, resin kit, unpainted; obsolete; less common. **$20 – 35**

Monogram (USA): Series 62 convertible, 1/20, plastic kit; usually red or light blue; obsolete; rare. Subject to bad warpage. **$35 – 150**

Monogram (USA): Coupe de Ville, 1/20, plastic kit; usually yellow; obsolete; rare. Subject to bad warpage. **$35 – 150**

Motor City (USA) MC-2: Fleetwood Series 60 Special sedan, 1/43, die-cast; metallic gray, burgundy, or white, with black top; obsolete; less common. Seems to be pantographed from Banthrico bank also. **$60 – 125**

Premier (USA): Eldorado convertible, 8¼", plastic kit; obsolete; rare. Early, crude kit; hardtop version also made; plated plastic trim parts. **$15 – 35**

Processed Plastics (USA): Series 62 convertible, 1/30, vinyl plastic; obsolete; less common. Snap-in wheels, snap-on windshield. **$10 – 20**

Processed Plastics (USA): Coupe de Ville, 1/30, vinyl plastic; obsolete; less common. One-piece body, snap-in wheels and windshield. **$10 – 20**

Revell/AMT (USA) H1200: Eldorado Biarritz convertible, 1/32, plastic kit, unpainted; obsolete; rare. **$30 – 100**

Ronnie's Ceramic Co. (USA): Coupe de Ville, 9", ceramic candy dish; two-tone pink; obsolete; rare. **$10 – 35**

Solido (France) 8011: Eldorado convertible (top-down), 1/18, die-cast; pink; current; common. **$10 – 35**

Solido (France) 8012: Eldorado convertible (top-up), 1/18, die-cast; metallic turquoise; current; common. **$10 – 35**

Structo (USA): Eldorado Brougham Motorama show car, 1/35, die-cast; obsolete; less common. From auto-transport set. Plated commemorative edition with decal available. **$8 – 25**

Zaugg (Switzerland) 9c: Series 62 hardtop, 1/43, resin/metal; red/white; current; less common. Low production, high price. **$80 – 250**

Zaugg (Switzerland) 9a: Series 62 convertible, 1/43, resin/metal; current; less common. Available factory-built or in kit form.
$60 – 200 (factory built); $30 – 60 (unbuilt kit)

1955 Eldorado convertibles, die-cast by Solido; doors open and wheels steer. Note lack of vent windows.

Two Zaugg die-casts: the Series 62 convertible and the Coupe de Ville

1956

The Automobile

Even though Cadillac's 1953 Orleans show car first explored the practicality of the four-door hardtop, it was not until 1956 that Cadillac added a new four-door hardtop Sedan de Ville. It became a runaway sales success. Another new body style was an Eldorado hardtop called the Seville. The Eldorado convertible became known as the Eldorado Biarritz. Horsepower was raised, the Hydramatic transmission was tweaked for crisper shifting, and styling sleight of hand made the 1956 bodies seem longer, lower, and wider than they really were.

Banthrico's slush-cast pot-metal 1956 Eldorado Sevilles; the pewter-finished 1980s reissue is at the top.

On the right: *Mercury's die-cast 1956 Eldorado convertible; Marco Bossi's copy in front of it includes the addition of Durham Classics whitewall replacement tires.*

1956 Eldorados. Notice how the snap-off hardtop changes the Biarritz into a Seville in these vinyl plastic models from Processed Plastics.

Monogram's kit for the 1956 Series 62 convertible, molded in nonwarping styrene

1956 in Miniature

Banthrico of Chicago made its last models/banks of contemporary cars in 1956. It was fitting that its last Cadillac was the dashing Eldorado Seville. Cast in pot metal and sporting the La Espada tail fins first seen in production on the 1955 Eldorado, this was the last hurrah for Banthrico Cadillacs. The success of AMT and Jo-Han in making flashy and accurately scaled plastic promotional models made it hard for the solid one-piece pot metal banks to compete for customers' attention. However, there is still a considerable following for original series Banthricos, and a good original example seldom brings less than a hundred dollars.

AMT's plastic promo of the 1956 Coupe de Ville

Banthrico changed management several times during the years since 1956, and the rediscovery of old molds led, in the 1970s, to the reissue of the 1956 Eldorado, along with the 1954 Series 60 Special, in unpainted bright pot metal. Both 1970s reisssues included the correct original-style black rubber tires. The easiest way to tell if an example is an original issue or a reproduction is to check the sheet-steel baseplate. Original issues have the keylock bank trap door. The reissues have only a blank baseplate, and sometimes a coin slot. Still another reissue was done in the 1980s, with oversized metal wheels and ugly antique pewter or brass finish. The unpainted reissue from the 1970s is preferable to the sloppy 1980s re-release.

Mercury of Italy offered a lovely 1/43 die-cast 1956 Eldorado Biarritz convertible in a variety of garish color schemes. Finely detailed grille, dash, upholstery pattern, and even correct "Sabre" wheels made this toy superior to any contemporary Dinky Toy or Corgi offerings. Sadly, Mercury never enjoyed the widespread distribution in America that Dinky or Corgi enjoyed, so these models are hard to find and command high prices.

In the late 1980s Marco Bossi of Italy marketed a limited edition of exact duplicates of the Mercury #28 Eldorado Biarritz, even down to the same baseplate markings. Distinguishing a copy from the original requires careful examination. Differences were three and easily overlooked. First, the copy's tires were black, rather than gray as on the original Mercury issue. Second, the copy's baseplate and bumpers were very shiny bare metal. Third, and most importantly, the original Mercury issue had axles that protruded through the centers of the Sabre-style wheels and were carefully peened to hold the wheel/tire assembly in place. The Bossi Sabre wheel had a solid center, and the axles were glued or press-fitted to the back of the wheel. However, both models are rare and highly desirable!

Miller Memorabilia handcast 1/25-scale 1956 Eldorado Seville and Eldorado Biarritz resin kits that were based on the Banthrico issues. The Miller version had accurate tires and hubcaps which added eye appeal and more realism.

Processed Plastics made a remarkably accurate vinyl plastic 1/43-scale sandbox toy Eldorado convertible with a mixture of 1955 and 1956 styling details and snap-in vinyl-plastic axles and wheels. Except for the thick, opaque windshield and lack of steering wheel necessitated by the body's one-piece molding process, this tiny toy was beautifully proportioned. Inexpensive and common for many years, this was a remarkable replica. A variation on the same mold added a snap-on hardtop to make it an Eldorado Seville.

The biggest and best 1956 Cadillac model was the Monogram (USA) 1/20-scale plastic kit. The option of the hardtop was omitted in 1956. While the 1955 Monogram Series 62 convertible was molded in the dreaded warping acetate, the 1956 version used glossy styrene that will never warp. Hence, the 1956 version is worth more today than the older 1955. With plated bumpers and glossy colored plastic body, this kit did not even really need painting except for fine detailing. Again, the factory-built sales samples are the most desirable examples, although any 1956 Monogram Cadillac is a rare find.

Revell and AMT teamed again in 1956 to make a fine 1/32-scale 1956 Eldorado Biarritz (convertible) plastic kit complete with plated parts, colorful box art, and happy driver and passenger figures. The awkward multi-piece body was still used to form the body shell, but the model was straightforward and easy to assemble. The lack of molded plastic window "glass" was the only disappointing omission for such a sophisticated plastic kit. Revell and AMT went their separate ways after this 1956 series of kits that included a Buick, Chrysler, Continental, Ford, and Mercury as well. Revell continued to use the multi-pieced body in its car kits while shortly thereafter AMT pioneered the one-piece molded car bodies used in their famous 1/25-scale "3-in-1" customizing kits and in production of some great promotional models.

AMT also made warp-prone acetate promotional, friction, and remote-control models of the 1956 Series 62 Coupe de Ville (with and without interiors) in 1/25-scale. Bumpers were plated cast metal, and the chassis were sheet steel. Whereas the 1955 examples had simulated raised side windows, the 1956 AMT coupes had "open" side windows. The acetate bodies eventually took on a "hunched" appearance as they shrank and pulled at their mountings on the steel chassis, thus bending and destroying the smooth Cadillac lines (and its value among collectors.) A nonwarped example is rare.

1956

AMT (USA): Coupe de Ville, 1/25, plastic promo; obsolete; rare. **$40 – 125**

Banthrico (USA): Eldorado Seville two-door hardtop, 1/25, original issue bank in pot metal, various colors; obsolete; very rare. **$90 – 200**

Banthrico (USA): Eldorado Seville two-door hardtop, 1/25, unpainted 1970s reissue; obsolete; rare. No lock in baseplate. **$25 – 50**

Banthrico (USA): Eldorado Seville, 1/25, pot metal, pewter finish; current; common; 1980s reissue. **$6 – 15**

Marco Bossi (Italy) 28: Eldorado convertible, 1/43, die-cast; obsolete; very rare. Mercury re-creation, almost impossible to tell from original, below. **$75 – 150**

Mercury (Italy) 28: Eldorado convertible, 1/43, die-cast; obsolete; very rare. **$100 – 200**

Miller Memorabilia (USA) 97: Eldorado Seville, 1/25, resin kit, unpainted; obsolete; less common. **$20 – 35**

Miller Memorabilia (USA): Series 62 convertible, 1/20, resin kit, unpainted; obsolete; less common. **$20 – 40**

1956 Eldorado convertible, as plastic kit from Revell

Monogram (USA): Series 62 convertible, 1/20, plastic (nonwarping styrene); usually red; obsolete; very rare.
$60 – 200

Processed Plastics (USA): Eldorado convertible, 1/43, vinyl plastic; obsolete; rare. One-piece body and interior with snap-in wheels, also snap-on Seville hardtop version.
$5 – 10

Revell/AMT (USA): Eldorado Biarritz convertible, 1/32, plastic kit; obsolete; unbuilt is very rare.
$30 – 100

1957

The Automobile

The Russians took the space high frontier in 1957 with the launching of Sputnik. American cars took the automotive-styling high frontier as they grew still longer, wider, and more powerful. A new X-shaped frame allowed the 1957 Cadillacs to be lower. The Eldorado Biarritz and Seville received new, distinctive rear-end treatments with sharklike fins that differed from those used on other lesser series. However, the flagship of the newly redesigned Cadillac line was the Motorama show

Left to right: *1957 Eldorado Sevilles, Galoob (Micromachine) plastic model and Elegance's handbuilt resin version; '57 Eldorado Broughams, in plastic from Galoob Micromachines and die-cast by Brooklin*

car-inspired Eldorado Brougham that met the Continental Mark II bumper to bumper in the high-priced luxo-specialty car market.

Since the Eldorado Brougham used many already familiar Cadillac styling motifs, few even noticed how special (and subtly different) this "production" car really was. Handmade on a separate special Fleetwood body assembly line, the Eldorado Brougham was actually a much larger car than it actually appeared. In addition, a sophisticated air-suspension system controlled by solenoids and valves literally pumped and floated the body on air. Quad headlights (still illegal in most states in 1957), air conditioning, brushed-stainless-steel roof, memory-position driver's seat, automatic trunk lid, signal-seeking radio, and special high-performance wide cross-section tires were standard. Startling center-opening doors revealed a posh interior with deep, rich mouton carpeting. Standard equipment included magnetized stainless drinking tumblers fitted to the glovebox door — as close to a dashboard-mounted in-car bar as Detroit was ever to offer in a "production" vehicle. A built-in makeup kit with complimentary Chanel No. 5 guaranteed that ladies looked and smelled lovely when they arrived at their destinations. Extravagant attention to detail was lavished upon this Cadillac luxo-flagship in order to bury the competition.

Although the elegant Continental Mark II was mechanically less sophisticated than the air-suspended Eldorado, its elegant lines seem less dated today. However, both cars set new standards for styling and quality for luxury cars of the era. The Continental listed at a whopping $9,517 while the Eldorado Brougham went for a staggering $13,074 — thousands more than lesser conventional offerings in their respective car lines. And, in turn, they were loss leaders for Ford and GM alike. With all of the painstaking hand work and extra steps involved to assure high quality control, both cars actually cost far more than their list prices to build, but Ford and GM were locked in a high-stakes game of posturing that was too expensive to continue for too long, and these distinctive cars' days were numbered from the start.

Still, it was a magnificent battle while it lasted!

1957 in Miniature

Auburn Rubber Company (USA) made a pliable vinyl-plastic 1⁄32-scale toy Eldorado Biarritz convertible with metal axles and white vinyl-plastic wheels. A chubby molded-in driver and passenger were poised for a long drive across the playroom floor. The opaque windshield and both front and rear bumpers were airbrushed silver, and the rear deck sported a nonstock, Chrysler Imperial-styled (?) continental kit. Somebody in the design department at Auburn Rubber Company must have shopped at J. C. Whitney! These squeezable toy boulevard cruisers were available for many years.

In the 1980s Elegance of France made a factory-finished, museum-quality resin model of the 1957 Eldorado Seville in 1⁄43 scale. Skillful use of photo-etched trim parts and decals for emblems made this a positive gem. Expensive and rare, this was the ultimate 1957 Eldorado Seville model.

Galoob currently offers two 1¼" Micromachine 1957 Cadillacs, a cartoonish Eldorado Seville and an Eldorado Brougham. Like most Micromachines, the little Cads have wheels and tires that look more suited to dune buggies. Great fun.

In the 1980s Playtoys of Belgium cast a fine 1⁄43-scale 1957 Eldorado Biarritz created (and signed) by famed model designer Carlo Brianza. Fine photo-etched grillework and a delicately folded cloth convertible top

Top: *Marx's 1957 Eldorado Brougham in plastic, presumed to be pantographed HO-scale copy of plastic Revell kit model, behind it.* ***Middle:*** *'57 Eldorado convertibles, with Carlo Brianza's handbuilt resin model to left of Auburn's vinyl.* ***Bottom:*** *TKM's resin kit of '57 Eldorado Seville, in primer paint and not yet detailed.*

make this detailed beauty one of the "Holy Grails" for miniature Cadillac collectors. Very expensive and hard to find!

For those who cannot find or afford the wonderfully finished Elegance and Playtoy models, Solido currently offers inexpensive mass-produced 1⁄43-scale versions of the Eldorado Biarritz, in convertible top-up (#4500) or top-down (#4501) configurations.

The Solido Eldorado's hood even opens to reveal a token plastic engine. To confound variation collectors, Solido makes the Eldorado convertible in a dizzying rainbow of colors. Recently, Solido added a new snap-on plastic roof that converts the Eldorado Biarritz casting into an Eldorado Seville. Again Solido uses the same baseplate and serial number, incorrectly identifying the Seville as a Biarritz. Another bothersome feature of the Solido Seville is the rear window. Apparently, in an effort to shave production costs, Solido uses the same clear plastic backlight as is used in the windshield. The unfortunate result is a tall rear window that upsets the subtle curve of the roof. This spoils an otherwise well-proportioned toy/model.

Marty Martino of Martino Miniatures (USA) designed a 1⁄43-scale resin 1957 Series 62 body-conversion kit for the Solido 1957 Eldorado #4500. The kit was briefly available through Miller Memorabilia. Modelers discarded the metal Solido Eldorado body and used the interior, windshield, baseplate, and chromed front bumper and wheels to create a Series 62 convertible with the Martino body.

TKM Models (USA) made a 1957 Eldorado Seville in a 1⁄25-scale cottage-industry resin kit. The detail was a little on the heavy side, but unmistakably Eldorado. Since the major kitmakers largely ignored the 1957 Cadillacs, TKM

***Top:** 1957 Eldorado Seville, Solido die-cast. **Middle:** Martino's resin '57 Series 62 (conversion kit for giving Solido Eldorado a new resin body) and the Solido die-cast. **Bottom:** Top-down and top-up versions of Solido's die-cast Eldorado convertible.*

models filled important gaps in a 1/25-scale Cadillac model collection. TKM also offered a Series 60 Special, and a Series 62 coupe and convertible.

Model-kit collectors covet the Revell 1/25-scale plastic kit of the 1957 Eldorado Brougham. Even though proportions were off, and there was no model engine under the model hood, this was and still is the only 1/25-scale version of this Cadillac classic, and it commands a high price built or unbuilt today. There is also a Marx Toys (Hong Kong) HO-scale pantographed copy that perfectly replicates all of the proportions, details, and flaws of the Revell 1/25-scale model. This tiny Eldorado Brougham came in a Marx Disney playset along with an HO-scale 1957 Ford Country Squire pantographed from yet another 1/25-scale Revell kit. It is unknown whether these cars were copied under license to Revell.

Brooklin Models of England makes a 1/43 factory-finished Eldorado Brougham that has captured the exotic flavor of the real car without getting it quite right. The metallic silver finish is deep, glossy, and most worthy of the 1957 Cadillac flagship. Proportions are off, but the Brougham's lines are subtle and not easy to capture in scale. Most striking on the car are the voluptuous "Dagmars" on the front bumper, the sweeping stainless lower body moldings, and the unique forged aluminum Brougham wheels. The Brooklin model has two glaring flaws. First, the Eldorado Brougham's distinctive brushed-stainless roof is neglected altogether. Second, the "ELDORADO" lettering on the trunk and hood is oversized to the point of cartoon exaggeration. Still, this is a desirable model that is currently available and well worth its moderate price.

1957

Auburn Rubber Co. (USA): Eldorado convertible, 1/32, vinyl plastic; usually red or yellow; obsolete; less common. **$8 – 12**

1958 60 Specials on an HO Southern Pacific auto loader (Lionel #0814200)

*1958 60 Specials. Jo-Han's friction-powered plastic **(top)** has normal acetate body warp; the Ex-El plastic promotional model **(bottom)** is a reproduction in nonwarping styrene plastic.*

Brooklin (GB) 27: Eldorado Brougham, 1⁄43, die-cast; silver; current; common. **$35 – 75**

Elegance (France) 121: Eldorado Seville, 1⁄43, resin; current; rare. Low production, high-priced handbuilt. **$125 – 350**

Galoob (China): Eldorado Seville, 1¼", plastic, orchid/white; current; common. Micromachine. **$.25 – 1**

Martino Miniatures (USA): Series 62 convertible, 1⁄43, resin body, unpainted (all other parts Solido); obsolete; rare. Special body conversion kit for Solido #4500 below. **$10 – 35**

Playtoys (Belgium): Eldorado Biarritz convertible, 1⁄43, resin/photo-etched trim; obsolete; rarest. Designed by Carlos Brianza and signed; low production, high price. **$150 – 350**

Revell (USA): Eldorado Brougham, 1⁄24, plastic kit; molded in black; obsolete; rare. **$100 – 200**

Solido (France) 4500: Eldorado Biarritz convertible (top-down), 1⁄43, die-cast; current; common. **$6 – 17**

Solido (France) 4501: Eldorado convertible (top-up), 1⁄43, die-cast; current; common. **$6 – 17**

Solido (France) 4520: Seville hardtop, 1⁄43, die-cast; current; common. Incorrect roof and rear window. **$6 – 17**

TKM (USA): Eldorado Seville, 1⁄25, unbuilt resin kit, unpainted; obsolete; less common. **$20 – 35**

Unknown (Hong Kong): Eldorado Brougham, HO, plastic; obsolete; rare. Pantographed from Revell 1⁄25 kit. **$7 – 15**

1958

The Automobile

While the automotive industry suffered a terrible sales slump during the 1958 recession, Cadillac suffered less due to its commanding market position. In addition, publication of *The Insolent Chariots* unleashed a broadside of scathing criticism of the auto industry. AMC's George Romney did not miss a chance to needle Detroit for continuing to build huge, gas-guzzling cars while increasing AMC Rambler sales seemed to indicate a fickle and changing market. Designers were scrambling into crash programs to build more compact, economical cars.

During 1958, flamboyant Harley Earl retired from GM after thirty years of service, and William Mitchell finally emerged from Earl's shadow to give new direction to GM styling. Changes were coming faster than most of the automakers could anticipate.

Cadillac management believed that the luxury market would continue to grow despite such recessions and purchased an old Hudson body plant from American Motors, in order to meet the growing demand for more Cadillacs. A whirlwind renovation program gave Cadillac modern, expanded, and improved facilities for 1958 at a fraction of the cost and headaches of building a completely new plant.

The Eldorado Brougham went into its second year of production but found few buyers, despite its uniqueness. However, it outlasted Ford's ambitious Continental Mark II, which died in August of 1957 from acute lack of sales. A pity!

1958 in Miniature

AHI Brand Toys (Japan) made a tiny, metal 1¾" Series 62 sedan in two-tone beige and brown. Crude and lacking plastic windows, this tiny pocket-sized Cadillac was best at home on an HO train layout where no one would look too closely at it. Tiny as it was, it had a die-cast body with a riveted tin chassis and rubber tires.

Jo-Han models (USA) made a 1⁄25-scale promotional model of the Series 60 Special in warp-prone acetate. The 60 Special's enormous anodized aluminum rear fender trim was simulated with silver paint. These models came with and without interiors and usually had friction motors. Promotional issues omitted the motors. Warped bodies, crazed windows, and melted hubcaps were all due to using the incompatible plastics on the same project, and such flaws keep collector prices down on all except the finest examples. Ex-El Products (USA) recovered the original molds and reissued the Jo-Han 1958 Cadillac in nonwarping styrene plastic in 1988. A compromise to missing or damaged dies forced Ex-El to use a 1959 dashboard and a crude new interior on the new issue. Even knowing this, a serious Cadillac collector should probably choose the reissued version to avoid the disfiguring warp of the original issues.

Lionel (USA) trains offered an HO-scale "auto-loader" train car that contained four different colored, plastic, HO-scale 1958 Series 60 Special sedans. These tiny Lionel Cadillacs, which have separate silver-painted bumpers and clear plastic windows, are not often seen.

Top: *Record's resin 1958 Series 62 Coupe de Ville and convertible, aftermarket Durham Classic whitewalls added.* ***Middle:*** *Eldorado Biarritz convertible and coupe, in resin by Record, again with whitewalls added.* ***Bottom:*** *Record resin '58 Sedan de Ville, Matchbox die-cast 60 Special, and AHI die-cast 60 Special.*

1958 Series 60 Special by Record

During the late 1950s Matchbox (Lesney) of England made a die-cast 2½" Series 60 Special sedan (#27) in metallic silver with a peach-colored roof. The tiny Cadillac had good proportions, fine bumper and grille detail, and plastic windows. Matchbox Cadillacs were made in large numbers, and this number should be easy to find at a Matchbox collectors' show.

French resin-modelmaker Record currently offers several 1958 Cadillacs in 1⁄43-scale, including an Eldorado Biarritz and Seville, a Series 62 convertible, Coupe and Sedan de Villes, and even a Series 60 Special. These models come painted and factory-assembled, but poorly detailed. Such lovely castings cry out for detailing to bring them up to a higher standard of finish. In 1991 Record also offered these models in unfinished kit form.

Since the 1957 and 1958 Eldorado Broughams were virtually identical, the descriptions under 1957 of the Galoob Micromachine, 1⁄25-scale Revell plastic kit, and the tiny HO-scale Marx Toys copy of the Revell kit would also apply here.

1958

AHI Brand Toys (Japan): Series 62 Sedan de Ville, HO, die-cast; beige/brown top; obsolete; less common. Crude body with tin chassis. **$4 – 8**

Jo-Han (USA): Series 60 Special four-door, 1⁄25, warp-prone plastic promo/friction; obsolete; rare. **$35 – 100**

Jo-Han/Ex-El (USA): Series 60 Special four-door sedan, 1⁄25, nonwarping styrene plastic; current; common. Reissue. **$15 – 35**

Lionel (USA): Series 60 Special four-door sedan, HO, plastic; red, black, blue, or white; obsolete; rare. From model railcar. **$8 – 15**

Matchbox (GB) 27: Series 60 Special four-door sedan, HO, die-cast; metallic silver/peach roof; obsolete; less common. **$20 – 50**

Record (France) 2: Eldorado Biarritz convertible, 1⁄43, resin body/die-cast chassis; current; less common. Also available in kit form. **$40 – 65**

Record (France) 4: Coupe de Ville, 1⁄43, resin body/die-cast chassis; current; common. Also available in kit form. **$40 – 65**

Record (France) 5: Sedan de Ville, 1⁄43, resin body/die-cast chassis; current; common. Also available in kit form. **$40 – 65**

Record (France) 6: Eldorado Seville, 1⁄43, resin body/die-cast chassis; current; common. Also available in kit form. **$40 – 65**

Record (France) 201: Series 60 Special, 1⁄43, resin body/die-cast chassis; current; common. Also available in kit form. **$40 – 65**

Record (France) 202: Series 62 convertible, 1⁄43, resin body/die-cast chassis; current; common. Also available in kit form. **$40 – 65**

1959

The Automobile

Whether loved or despised, Cadillac's 1959 styling was the high point of the tail fin era. In truth, Cadillac's outrageous 38"-high fin was penned in knee-jerk reaction to the boldness of Chrysler's "Forward Look" of 1957, and the tail fin never attained such dizzying nosebleed heights again. Indeed, all General Motors divisions probably offered the public more variations on the tail fin in 1959 than ever dreamed possible. Nonetheless, rocketship Cadillac styling was not rejected by the public, and some 142,000 new Cadillacs were purchased. Distinctive body sculpture, fantastic flights of chrome, and enormous compound curved windshields gave individual GM divisions identities that made 1959 styling a milestone. The need to maintain such division identities would be an expensive lesson for GM to relearn in the 1980s.

At the 1959 opening of the Daytona Speedway, Harley Earl's last dream car — the Cadillac Cyclone — powered through some demonstration laps before the beginning of the race. The Cyclone was the ultimate incarnation of the Cape Canaveral school of car design, for it packed its own collision-avoidance radar system, a jet-fighter-style bubble canopy, simulated jet-nozzle taillights, and wild shark fins. Even though Cadillac had no intention of building such road-rocket sports cars, the race fans gathered at Daytona loved it!

Production of the Eldorado Brougham was turned over to Pinanfarina in Italy, and only ninety-nine new 1959 Eldorado Broughams were built. The new Brougham was based on a larger body than before with more standard production Cadillac underpinnings to cut costs. Perhaps the fact that the new Brougham was less distinctive than

Top: *1959 Cadillac "Ecto 1A" Ghostbusters staff car as an AMT kit and the cartoonish die-cast "Ectomobile" available from Columbia Pictures, shown in and out of the special Fuji film packaging.* ***Bottom:*** *Kenner's plastic "Ectomobile".*

1959 60 Special, pressed steel from Bandai

the 1957-1958 editions caused its even more disappointing sales, or perhaps Cadillac just kept the Brougham around for another year to tweak Ford's corporate nose after the demise of the Continental Mark II. Such posturing carried a high price tag, but Cadillac apparently thought it had the last word.

1959 in Miniature

In the breaking wave of nostalgia for 1950s rock and roll and fashion, the 1959 Cadillac has emerged as a new American icon. Models of the 1959 Cadillac are many, but the Eldorado Brougham and zoomy Cyclone are not among them.

The successful *Ghostbusters* movies of the 1980s glamorized the refurbished 1959 Cadillac ambulance used to track troublesome spirits, and in the spring of 1990 AMT released a 1⁄25-scale plastic kit of it dubbed the "Ecto 1A." This is an all-new mold and an interesting kit with all of the strange ghost-hunting equipment included.

Kenner's (USA) roughly 1⁄18-scale red and white plastic (cartoon) version of the ghostbusters' Caddy features opening doors and free-rolling wheels. Designed to accept play figures from the movie/cartoon series, this impressionistic interpretation of a 1959 Caddy is still available. Columbia Pictures also gave away a die-cast 2¾" version of the same cartoon vehicle in special multi-roll packs of Fuji camera film.

AHI Brand Toys (Japan) made a tiny 1¾" Coupe de Ville in die-cast metal with a riveted tin chassis and rubber tires. Detail was crude, and the toy lacked plastic windows. This tiny, blue, toy Cadillac is often overlooked.

Tin toy manufacturer Bandai (Japan) made an 11" Fleetwood 60 Special sedan from pressed steel. This was an inexpensive toy, but it is now being discovered by collectors. Prices are rising quickly on most Japanese "tin." A four-door (?) convertible version of this toy was also made, leading one to believe that the manufacturer simply cut down the sedan in order to offer an additional variation without proper retooling.

Virginia modeler Marty Martino commissioned the revived Banthrico to copy his pattern for a 1⁄25-scale 1959 Eldorado Biarritz. Unlike the older series Banthrico car banks, which were painted and rubber-tired, this recent issue had metal wheels and tires, a vinyl plastic pop-in bank door in the chassis, and an unattractive antique brass finish. Heavy grinding of the fins played havoc with the details Martino sought to include on an otherwise nice

1959 Eldorado Biarritz convertible coin bank, antique brass finish on pot metal by Marcast/Banthrico

Dinky die-cast 1959 Coupe de Villes: red and white was the first issue, pink and white the second.

toy/model. A number of these banks were sold under Martino's "Marcast" label, and a sticker with the "MM" logo appeared on the chassis.

Matchbox International revived the Dinky name in 1988, and one of its initial offerings was a 1/43-scale 1959 Cadillac Series 62 coupe. Well-proportioned, reasonably well-made, and popularly priced, this is a desirable current offering that carries on the tradition of quality at a low price established by the old Dinky Toy line.

Gunze Sangyo (Japan) offered 1/32-scale plastic kits of the 1959 Eldorado Biarritz and Eldorado Seville. Both were easy to build and could be adapted to accept electric motors. Revell (USA) now offers the Gunze Sangyo Cadillac Eldorado Biarritz kit under its own label, but it is the same kit. Alloy Forms, a company specializing in train layout items, offered a "white" metal HO-scale pantographed copy of the Gunze Sangyo Cadillac Eldorado Biarritz in kit or factory-assembled (and painted) form.

Franklin Mint distributes a handsome 1/43-scale die-cast 1959 Eldorado Biarritz convertible in its "Cars of the Fifties" series. Built overseas by Chinese craftsman, it features opening hood and doors, as well as the dramatic sweep of chrome body trim that was exclusive to the Eldo. This is a nice model for the money, and it captures the flamboyance of the real car very well.

Jo-Han (USA) offered a 1/25-scale promotional 1959 Cadillac Fleetwood sedan model in warp-prone acetate plastic. Although done in pleasing colors and factory assembled, these models warped, crazed, and deteriorated badly with time. A better bet is to find the same car molded in nonwarping styrene plastic as used in Jo-Han's plastic model kits. Unfortunately, an unbuilt Jo-Han 1959 Cadillac kit is very rare; it will probably cost much more than the assembled promotional model. Ex-El Products has since rediscovered the original molds used for the promo and kit and reissued it in nonwarping styrene plastic, all factory assembled. Emblems, trim, and interior details have suffered in the reissue; this mold must have been well worn. These new issues sell at collectors' prices but are still less than the price of an original kit or promotional.

1959 Eldorado Biarritz convertible made from Gunze Sanyo's plastic kit, with boxed kit of their Eldorado Seville coupe

Galoob (China) makes a variety of tiny free-rolling cartoonish vehicles averaging about an inch long. Micromachines included in several sets are a version of the Eldorado Biarritz convertible and a bizarre Series 75 limo. These are far more toys than models, but they merit mention.

Popworks (Korea) makes a large 20" x 9" boombox stereo tape player/radio that looks like the rear end sawed off a Series 62 convertible! The bullet taillights flash, and the tape deck and radio tuner are under the trunk lid. This stereo was featured in the Sharper Image Christmas catalog in 1989, and it operates on the owner's choice of batteries or household current.

Mattel Hot Wheels (Malaysia) offers a Series 62 convertible in pearl white with red interior. A Canadian version is painted pink.

Miller Memorabilia offered a Series 60 Special in a 1/25-scale resin kit with vacuum-formed clear plastic windows and interior. This cottage-industry model was handcast to order.

Model Auto Emporium (Canada) makes a factory-finished, 1/43-scale, die-cast Series 62 convertible in top-up (#101) and top-down (#102) versions. These are heavy and relatively well-detailed models at healthy prices. The only real weakness is the rear bumper, which seems poorly proportioned. Nonetheless, this is a quality model.

"Mr. Sandman's 1950s Dream Machines" (honest!) of Canada makes one of the most unusual 1959 Cadillac convertible models out of a mixture of glue, glitter, and pink sand (pictured in the Introduction to this book). Although it is labeled as an Eldorado, it lacks the Eldo chrome side trim and emblems. Pudgy and comically bloated, this hefty 8" fugitive from beach gift shops could readily be pressed into service as a doorstop if need be. A smaller 4" version is also available. Definitely a must-have for the Cadillac kitsch collection!

Palmer Plastics built a particularly bad 1959 Eldorado Biarritz convertible. The factory-built store displays were so ugly that retailers often discarded them, hoping potential modelers would then be fooled by the much nicer art on the kit box.

Road Champs (China) offers a 3" die-cast convertible with snap-on boot or raised roof as part of a boxed set of

*Note opening hood and doors of the Franklin Mint die-cast 1959 Eldorado Biarritz convertible (shown front view, **below**, and rear, **left**); Vitesse brought out a "Just Married" version of the '59 Series 62 convertible, complete with driver, bride and groom, graphics, and tiny chromed pots and pans dragging from the rear bumper.*

1959 60 Special as plastic promo reissued by Ex-El and as Jo-Han's plastic kit model

Left and right: *Popworks' 1959 Cadillac trunk opens to reveal radio and tape deck.*

American cars from the 1950s. The Chinese must have a sense of humor, for they silkscreened the words "Big Fins" on the rear fenders.

Telemania of China manufactures a surprisingly handsome 10½" model of an Eldorado Seville that is also a telephone. When the car phone rings, the headlights and bullet taillights flash, and the horn honks! The shipping box incorrectly indicates that the phone is modeled after an Eldorado Biarritz, but its hardtop actually makes it a Seville. Available in pink/white and black/white, this is a must-see for Caddy buffs.

Vitesse (Portugal) makes a factory-finished, 1⁄43-scale, die-cast 1959 Series 62 convertible with a plastic chassis and interior. These are reasonably priced collector models, but they are not perfect. The collector has to glue on door handles and mirrors, and the tail fins seem to be oversized wings better suited to the Batmobile. However, this is a current issue not to be missed.

A wacky 1991 Christmas offering is a hefty 14" Regal China 1959 Cadillac convertible Jim Beam bourbon decanter. While the plated bumpers and windshield trim are excellent plastic castings, the bottle body is a complex molded affair glazed in a shocking pink that would make Mary Kay Ashe blush with delight. The bottle opening and cap are cleverly concealed under the plastic top-down convertible boot, and body side trim and emblems are stick-on labels and chromed tape. The whole affair rolls (and sloshes) nicely on handsome white-wall tires with fully chromed wheel covers. While this is not a dead accurate car model, it is strikingly attractive and weirdly wonderful.

1959

AHI Brand Toys (Japan): Series 62 Coupe de Ville, HO, die-cast body/tinplate chassis; blue; obsolete; less common. **$4 – 8**

*Top: 1959 Series 62 convertibles, die-cast by Vitesse and by Model Auto Emporium (note different interpretations). **Bottom:** 1959 Series 75 custom limousine, plastic Galoob Micromachine; Series 62 convertible, die-cast by Road Champs, with opening doors and interchangeable top boot or raised convertible roof; Eldorado Biarritz convertible, die-cast from Alloy Forms kit, presumed to have been pantographed from larger Gunze Sangyo plastic kit; and Coupe de Ville, AHM die-cast.*

*Road Champs' 1959 convertible stock version **(left)** and the Hot Wheels version **(right)**; behind them, the stock version has truly become a monster car.*

Alloy Forms (USA): Eldorado Biarritz convertible, HO, "white" metal, unpainted; obsolete; less common. Tiny kit pantographed from Gunze Sangyo model, below. **$4 – 8**

AMT/Ertl (USA) 6017: Ghostbusters' ambulance, 1⁄25, plastic kit, unpainted; current; common. **$5 – 12**

Bandai (Japan): Fleetwood 60 Special four-door, 11", "tin"; obsolete; rare. Friction drive; a cut-down convertible version is also derived from the same body. **$75 – 200**

Banthrico (USA): Eldorado Biarritz convertible, 1⁄25, pot metal; antique bronze tone; obsolete; less common. 1980s issue Banthrico designed by Marty Martino. **$12 – 25**

Columbia Pictures (China): Ghostbusters' ambulance, 2¾", die-cast; white/red; obsolete; less common. Cartoonish. **$4 – 15 (with Fuji film pack)**

Dinky (revival by Matchbox, GB): Series 62 coupe, 1⁄43, die-cast; red/white; obsolete; common. **$10 – 20**

Dinky (revival by Matchbox, GB): Series 62 coupe, 1⁄43, die-cast; pink/white; current; common **$10 – 17**

Franklin Mint (USA): Eldorado convertible, 1⁄43, die-cast; white; current; common. Cars of the Fifties Series. By subscription. **$35 – 60**

Galoob (China): Series 75 limousine, 2", plastic; silver; current; common. Micromachine. **$.25 – 1**

*1959 Eldorado Seville phone **(right)**, Series 62 calculator **(left)** and a Series 62 convertible, which is really a Jim Beam bottle*

Vitesse's die-cast 1959 Series 62 convertibles, top-down and top-up versions

Galoob (China): convertible, 1", solid plastic; current; common. Cartoonish interpretation. **$.25 – 1**

Gunze Sangyo (Japan): Eldorado Biarritz convertible, 1/32, plastic kit; red, yellow, or blue; obsolete; common. Also sold under Revell name. **$6 – 17**

Gunze Sangyo (Japan): Eldorado Seville, 1/32, plastic kit; obsolete; less common. **$6 – 17**

Jim Beam (USA): Series 62 convertible, 14", china decanter bottle; current; common. **$75 – 110**

Jo-Han (USA): Fleetwood four-door, 1/25; plastic kit, unpainted; obsolete; rare. **$60 – 150**

Jo-Han (USA): Fleetwood four-door sedan, 1/25, warp-prone plastic; obsolete; very rare. Friction drive. **$60 – 90**

Jo-Han/Ex-El (USA): Fleetwood four-door, 1/25; plastic; current; common. Reissue of promo/friction done in non-warping plastic. **$15 – 40**

Kenner (USA): Ghostbusters' ambulance, 1/18 (?), plastic; red/white; current; common. For cartoon action figures. **$5 – 25**

Marksman (China): 1959 Cadillac calculator, 5" x 1 3/4", plastic; pink or black; current; less common. Looks like rear fenders, bumper, trunk lid, and fins from rear of 1959 Cadillac; you lift trunk lid to expose keys and LCD readout. **$10 – 25**

Mattel Hot Wheels (Malaysia): 1959 Series 62 convertible, 3 3/8", die-cast/plastic trim; pearl white; current; common. **$1 – 3**

Mattel Hot Wheels (Malaysia): 1959 Series 62 convertible, 3⅜", die-cast/plastic trim; pink; current; less common Canadian version with graphics. **$5 – 15**

Miller Memorabilia (USA) CC55B: Series 69 four- door hardtop, 1⁄25, resin kit, unpainted; obsolete; less common. **$25 – 40**

Model Auto Emporium (Canada) 101: Series 62 convertible (top-up), 1⁄43, die-cast; current; common. **$45 – 80**

Model Auto Emporium (Canada) 102: Series 62 convertible (top-down), 1⁄43, die-cast; current; common. **$45 – 80**

Mr. Sandman's 1950s Dream Machines (Canada): convertible, 8", pressed, glued and molded sand; pink; current; common. Gift shop item. **$3 – 10**

Palmer (USA): Eldorado Biarritz convertible, 1⁄25, plastic kit, unpainted; obsolete; rare. **$10 – 20**

Popworks (Korea) 3-1489: 1959 Cadillac boombox stereo radio and tape player; 20" x 9" plastic; pink or black; current; less common. Looks like rear fender, bumper, trunk lid, and fins from rear of 1959 Cadillac. **$100 – 200**

Revell (USA) H1200: Eldorado Biarritz convertible, 1⁄32, plastic kit; current; common. Reissue of Gunze Sangyo kit, above. **$5 – 12**

Road Champs (China): convertible, 3", die-cast; red; common. "Big Fins" silkscreened on rear fenders. **$1 – 5**

Telemania (China): 1959 Eldorado Seville telephone, 10½", plastic, pink/white or black/white; current; common. Incorrectly labeled a Biarritz. **$20 – 60**

Vitesse (Portugal) 380: Series 62 convertible (top-down), 1⁄43, die-cast/plastic trim; current; common. **$12 – 25**

Vitesse (Portugal) 381: Series 62 convertible (top-up), 1⁄43, die-cast/plastic trim; current; common. **$12 – 25**

Vitesse (Portugal) 382: Series 62 convertible (top-down), 1⁄43, die-cast/plastic trim; current; common. "Just Married" graphics and figures of bride and groom with driver. **$12 – 25**

Vitesse (Portugal) 383: Series 62 Coupe de Ville, 1⁄43, die-cast/plastic trim; current; common. **$12 – 25**

1960 Sedan de Villes. ***Foreground:*** *Tootsietoy die-cast.* ***Background, left to right:*** *Two die-cast variations from Lone Star and a smaller Tootsietoy.*

1960

The Automobile

The battle for the compact car market occupied much attention in auto circles during 1960, but Cadillac motored on in fine fashion, concerned with the other end of the auto spectrum. The flamboyant excesses of 1959 styling were refined, and the outrageous tail fins were trimmed. Use of chrome trim was more restrained when compared to the previous year's Cadillac, except for that used on the glitzy Eldorado Biarritz and Seville. This was to be the Eldorado Seville's last year as well as the Pinanfarina-built Eldorado Brougham's final handmade Italian edition of a mere hundred units. Pinanfarina would not be involved in Cadillac production again for twenty-seven years, until the introduction of the 1987 Allante.

Competing Lincoln and Chrysler Imperial offerings did not age as well through their restyling cycles. The huge uni-body Lincoln looked bulky and bloated with a body little changed since its 1958 introduction, and the third restyling of the 1957 Imperial body lacked the elegant lines of the Cadillac. Cadillac was still America's luxury leader.

1960 in Miniature

Bandai toymakers of Japan made an 11" tin Sedan de Ville with a friction motor. An alternate version was a four-door convertible (?) made from a cut-down Sedan de Ville.

Jo-Han made 1/25-scale plastic promotional and friction models in warp-prone acetate. These were attractive models that came in authentic colors, but shrinking and distortion twisted the bodies into strange shapes. This hurt the value of these models. Collectors seek the original Jo-Han plastic kit of the 1960 Cadillac. It was from the same basic mold, but it was cast in polystyrene that will not warp. Beginning with the 1960 Jo-Hans, all Cadillac promos, frictions, and kits were equipped with interiors.

Lone Star Roadmasters of England made a medium blue, 1/50-scale, die-cast Series 62 sedan with windows, an interior, white tires, and dull silver plastic bumpers. An alternate version of the Lone Star Roadmasters Series 62 sedan eliminated the interior and added die-cast metal bumpers, chromed wheel hubs, black tires, and a

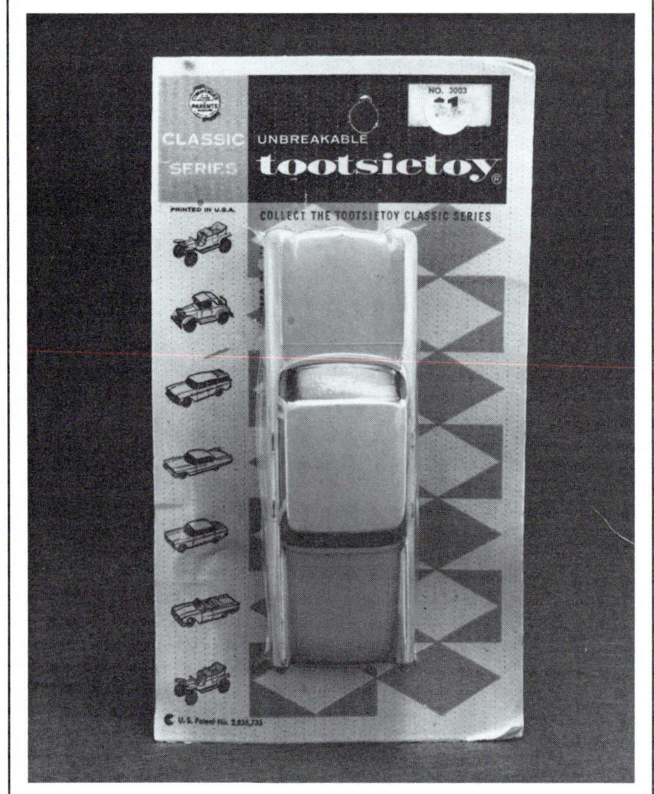

Using blister-pack cards is one economical way of marketing models; here, a Tootsietoy '60 Sedan de Ville.

Bandai's pressed-steel 1960 Sedan de Ville

1960 60 Special from Jo-Han's plastic kit

cream-colored roof. The baseplate and body were otherwise the same. Still another variation of this same casting (manufactured in England) was licensed to Tootsietoy (USA). It was light blue with cream top, had no interior, and sported metal bumpers and wheel hubs. "Tootsietoy Classic Series" was molded in raised letters on the black baseplate. The Tootsietoy version was sold on a shrink-wrapped blister card while the Lone Star Roadmaster came in a cardboard box.

Miller Memorabilia offered a handcast 1⁄25-scale resin model kit of Series 60 Special four-door sedan.

Yonezawa (Japan) made an 18" tin 1960 Fleetwood 60 Special. The major flaw was the 1959 side trim on the 1960 body. Such tin toys are eagerly sought by toy collectors today. Expect to pay a high price.

1960

Bandai (Japan): Sedan de Ville, 11", "tin"; obsolete; very rare. Friction drive; also available, a cut-down four-door convertible from same body. **$75 – 175**

Jo-Han (USA) 2860: Fleetwood four-door, 1⁄25, plastic kit, unpainted; obsolete; very rare. **$60 – 150**

Jo-Han (USA): Fleetwood four-door hardtop, 1⁄25, warping acetate; obsolete; rare. Friction or promo. **$45 – 100**

Lone Star Roadmasters (GB): Series 62 sedan, 1⁄50, die-cast; medium blue; obsolete; rare. Dull silver plastic bumpers, full interior tub, white tires. **$20 – 45**

Lone Star Roadmasters (GB): Series 62 sedan, 1⁄50, die-cast; darker blue than Tootsietoy, below; obsolete; less common. Same as Tootsietoy version, only different baseplate and color. **$20 – 45**

Miller Memorabilia (USA) CC56B: Series 60 four-door hardtop, 1⁄25, resin kit, unpainted; obsolete; less common. **$25 – 45**

Politoy (Italy): Eldorado Brougham, 1⁄43, die-cast; dark blue; obsolete; rare. **$45 – 90**

Tootsietoy (GB) 3003: Series 62 sedan, 1⁄50, die-cast; light blue/cream; obsolete; less common. Tootsietoy Classic Series; possibly Lone Star design under license, or vice versa. **$20 – 45**

Yonezawa (Japan): Fleetwood 60 Special, 18", "tin"; black/white trim; obsolete; rarest. Friction; actually 1959 rear fender trim, not correct. **$400 – 800**

1961

The Automobile

Cadillac was settling into the Mitchell era, and the voluptuous curves so favored by the Harley Earl school were eased out of GM new product design. It seems that the lean and lithe 1960 Eldorado Brougham served as the initial inspiration for the all-new 1961 line-up that sported new knife-edged sculpturing. In a bold move, Cadillac also chose to reduce the size of the car. The public was not ready for a down-sized Cadillac at that time, but the lighter car handled and even stopped better than its 1960 counterpart. Even though Lincoln fielded a critically acclaimed new sedan and four-door convertible for 1961, Cadillac still readily outsold both Lincoln and Imperial again. Winning momentum was on Cadillac's side once again.

1961 in Miniature

Anguaplas Minicars of Spain made a tiny HO-scale Fleetwood Series 75 limousine with opening passenger doors. Unfortunately, it was molded in warping plastic, and it distorted badly with age.

Dinky of England made a die-cast metallic dark turquoise Series 62 sedan that featured interior, clear plastic windows, and even a spring suspension! Although the greenhouse area was a little exaggerated, it was a pleasing 1⁄43-scale model. Strange variations on the Dinky Cadillac were a black and white American-style police cruiser and a dark blue Royal Canadian Mounted Police patrol car complete with dome light and two mounties. One wonders just what the Brits thought was going on in North American police equipment procurement. Probably the Dinky Toy people found themselves in need of a base vehicle for a police car, and the Cadillac was new and exciting and available.

Jo-Han made a plastic 1⁄25-scale promotional model of the 1961 Fleetwood Series Special. Unfortunately, Jo-Han again used warp-prone acetate plastic. A better choice was the kit version, which was molded in nonwarping polystyrene. Jo-Han frequently used glossy pastel-colored plastics in its model kits, so an unpainted but polished kit can be confused with an unwarped promotional model unless the collector is familiar with kit-style wheels and axles.

Korris Kars (USA) made what seemed to be a 1⁄25-scale vinyl-plastic copy of the Jo-Han promotional model. The

Top: *1/43 American and RCMP police cars, based on 1961 Cadillacs, die-cast by Dinky Toy.* ***Bottom:*** *Dinky Toy's die-cast 1961 Sedan de Ville and a HO Series 75 limousine in plastic by Anguaplas.*

The 1961 60 Special vinyl plastic on the right is presumed to have been pantographed by Korris Kars from the Jo-Han kit next to it, or from a promo model. Chassis details are pictured in the Introduction to this book.

Korris version lacked the chassis plate and had snap-in wheels with chrome foil hubcaps!

Miller Memorabilia offered a 1/25-scale resin Fleetwood Series 60 Special sedan handcast in resin to order.

Palmer (USA) made a low-quality 1/32-scale 1961 Eldorado Biarritz plastic kit. With its primitive generic chassis and wheels and multi-piece body, this kit was simply not up to the same standards as the Jo-Han model. Prices remain low for even mint, unbuilt examples.

SSS of Japan made a large 17½" tin Fleetwood Series 75 with friction drive. This was a fine example of Japanese tin toy design and commands high prices today.

Cadillac kitsch was represented by a Windsor 1/20-scale die-cast Coupe de Ville that served as combination cigarette box/lighter desk set. The gold(?)-plated roof and greenhouse lifted off the gold-plated body shell to reveal a well to store cigarettes. A huge lighter nested in a circular hole in the trunk lid — a sort of bizarre continental kit.

1961

Anguaplas (Spain) 86: Series 75 Fleetwood limousine, 1/86, plastic; obsolete; less common. Warps badly; opening passenger doors. **$2 – 5**

Dinky Toys (GB) 147: Series 62 four-door sedan, 1/43, die-cast; metallic blue/green; obsolete; rare. Stock version. **$35 – 100**

Dinky Toys (GB) 147: Series 62 sedan, 1/43, die-cast; dark blue; obsolete; rare. RCMP police car. **$35 – 100**

Dinky Toys (GB) 147: Series 62 sedan, 1/43, die-cast; black; obsolete; rare. American police car. **$35 – 100**

Jo-Han (USA): Fleetwood Series 60 Special four-door, 1/25, warping plastic; obsolete; rare. Friction. **$35 – 100**

Jo-Han (USA): Fleetwood Series 60 Special four-door, 1/25, plastic kit; obsolete; rare. **$45 – 125**

Korris Kars (USA): Fleetwood four-door, 1/25, vinyl plastic; obsolete; rare. Copy of Jo-Han promo body. **$20 – 40**

Miller Memorabilia (USA) CC58B: Fleetwood Series 60 four-door sedan, 1/25, resin kit, unpainted; obsolete; less common. **$25 – 40**

Palmer (USA) 6173: Eldorado Biarritz, 1/32, plastic kit, unpainted; obsolete; rare. Inferior kit; multi-piece body. **$5 – 15**

SSS (Japan): Fleetwood Series 75, 17½", "tin"; cream; obsolete; rarest. Friction drive. **$200 – 500**

Windsor (Japan): Coupe de Ville, 1/20, metal; gold-plated; obsolete; rare. Cigarette box with lighter. **$40 – 100**

Palmer's kit for a plastic 1961 Eldorado Biarritz convertible with Windsor's die-cast plated cigarette box and lighter set

1962

The Automobile

Cadillac celebrated its sixtieth anniversary in 1962. George Jetson and his futuristic cartoon family made their first TV appearance that same year. George would have loved the 1962 Cadillac, for it embodied the sleek American rocket-age technology of the 1960s and promised performance and comfort for its proud owner.

Tastefully finned and adorned with new grille, cornering lights, and a new dual master-cylinder braking system, the mildly restyled Cadillac enjoyed increased sales while Lincoln and Imperial tried to loosen GM's grip on the American luxury-car market with their own minor styling changes.

Life was good at Cadillac.

1962 in Miniature

Corgi of England offered a 1/43-scale die-cast 1962 Cadillac Superior Ambulance. A tiny battery cassette inserted in the chassis flashed the dome light. Great fun, but no siren! Parents liked this one.

Jo-Han made a 1/25-scale plastic Fleetwood Series 60 Special in both promotional and kit form. Again, the kit was molded in nonwarping polystyrene and remains preferable to the warp-prone promo model.

Miller Memorabilia sold a 1/25-scale resin kit of a 1962 Fleetwood Series 60 Special handcast to order.

Jo-Han's plastic kit for 1962 60 Special

Top: *Variations on Corgi's die-cast 1962 Cadillac Superior Ambulances (note the battery-powered flashing dome light).* ***Bottom:*** *Rare '62 60 Special, in plastic by Politoy (note opening front doors) (all from Ferd Zegel Collection).*

Die-cast toymaker Politoys of Italy made a 5¼" plastic-bodied 60 Special in odd 1⁄41 scale. This appears to be one of a short-lived series of early 1960s American cars done in this unusual scale. Very rare.

Yonezawa of Japan made a huge 22" tin Fleetwood Series 60 Special with a friction motor. Japanese tin in good shape is hard to find and commands high prices today.

1962

Corgi (GB): Superior Ambulance, 1⁄43, die-cast; white/blue or red/cream; obsolete; rare. Battery-powered flashing emergency lights. **$35 – 100**

Jo-Han (USA): Fleetwood Series 60 Special, 1⁄25, warp-prone plastic; obsolete; rare. Friction. **$40 – 90**

Jo-Han (USA): Fleetwood four-door, 1⁄25, nonwarping polystyrene plastic kit; obsolete; rare. **$35 – 100**

Miller Memorabilia (USA) CC59B: Fleetwood Series 60 Special four-door hardtop, 1⁄25, resin kit, unpainted; obsolete; less common. **$25 – 40**

Politoy (Italy) 69: Series 60 Special, 1⁄41, plastic; light blue; obsolete; very rare. Opening front doors. **$35 – 100**

Yonezawa (Japan): Fleetwood 60 Special, 22", "tin"; red; obsolete; rarest. Friction. **$200 – 500**

1963

The Automobile

The biggest news for Cadillac in 1963 was the new V-8 to replace the old 331-cid V-8 first introduced in 1949. The old V-8 had been bored out, tweaked, and massaged to 390-cid and 325-horsepower over a successful production run of fourteen years. As a further refinement, the new 1963 Cadillac switched from a generator to a modern Delco alternator. Interiors offered an adjustable steering wheel, and even an AM/FM radio. Styling boasted

*1963 Series 62 convertibles. **Top to bottom:** Friction-powered plastic, manufacturer unknown; same as above but with plated body and built-in battery-powered AM radio in chassis, also unknown manufacturer; and plastic kit model by Jo-Han.*

__Top:__ 1963 Sedan de Ville die-cast by Windsor in form of gold-plated cigarette box and lighter set. __Bottom:__ Its 1964 model cousin.

smaller fins and extended front fenders to give the impression of Gilbraltar-like solidity; Cadillac offered the ultimate American dream machine once again. Conspicuous consumption was hip!

1963 in Miniature

Bandai toymakers of Japan made a 17" tin toy 1963 Cadillac convertible and a 17" tin Series 60 Special — each powered by a friction motor.

Prolific Franklin Mint (USA) discovered a market for highly detailed 1/43-scale collectible model cars with its 1989 series of "Cars of the Sixties," a spin-off from its successful "Cars of the Fifties" series. Available by mail order, these Chinese-made models are colorful and feature opening hoods and doors. Of special interest to model Cadillac collectors is the handsome metallic blue 1963 Eldorado Biarritz convertible. Franklin Mint outlet stores have been known to break up sets to sell individual cars separately, but the complete set also includes a wooden shelf display and a book of colorful ad reproductions for the series cars.

Jo-Han (USA) made 1/25-scale plastic promotional models of the Coupe de Ville and convertible, as well as 1/25-scale plastic model kits. The 1963 Cadillac model kits were the first Jo-Han kit Cads to have opening hoods and model engines.

An unknown Hong Kong toymaker pantographed the 1/25-scale Jo-Han Caddy convertible into larger 1/20-scale and added a chassis containing an AM radio. Volume and tuning knobs were located beneath the front bumper, while speaker and battery box tucked neatly out of sight in the chassis. Except for garish colors and some sloppy assembly work, this could have passed as a decent 1/20-scale promotional model. Inexplicably, the body shell was dark chrome-plated while bumpers and hubcaps

This die-cast 1963 Eldorado convertible is part of Franklin Mint's "Cars of the Sixties" series.

were gold-plated! Another version from the same mold lacked the AM radio and bizarre plated body shell. It substituted a friction motor and sported more conventional-looking chrome-plated bumpers and hubcaps.

Close cousin to the gold(?)-plated Windsor 1961 Cadillac cigarette case/lighter model was a 1963 version of the Sedan de Ville. Like the 1961 model, the removable roof revealed storage for cigarettes while the trunk lid sported a lift-out lighter. How wonderfully tacky!

1963

Bandai (Japan): de Ville convertible, 17", "tin"; white; obsolete; rarest. **$150 – 450**

Bandai (Japan): Fleetwood Series 60 Special, 17", "tin"; gold; obsolete; rarest. Friction. **$150 – 450**

Franklin Mint (USA): Eldorado Biarritz convertible, 1/43, die-cast/plastic; light metallic blue; current; common. "Cars of the Sixties" set, made in China. **$25 – 60**

Jo-Han (USA): Coupe de Ville, 1/25, plastic kit; obsolete; rare. **$15 – 45**

Jo-Han (USA): Coupe de Ville, 1/25, plastic promo; obsolete; rare. **$45 – 75**

Jo-Han (USA): de Ville convertible, 1/25, plastic promo; obsolete; rare. **$45 – 100**

Jo-Han (USA) 4363: de Ville convertible, 1/25, plastic kit; obsolete; rare. **$15 – 45**

Unknown (Hong Kong): de Ville convertible, 1/20, plastic; gold trim/plated body; obsolete; less common. AM radio with battery box in chassis; same body as #R 4410, below. **$20 – 45**

Unknown (Hong Kong) R 4410: Series 62 convertible, 1/20, plastic; gray/red interior; plastic; obsolete; rare. Pantographed from Jo-Han promo in 1/20 scale; friction motor. **$40 – 90**

Windsor (Japan) 2: Series 62 de Ville four-door sedan, 8⅝", die-cast; gold-plated; obsolete; rare. Cigarette box with lighter in trunk cut-out. **$40 – 100**

1964

The Automobile

There was new attention paid to courting the rising class of professionals who could afford to move up to Cadillac. An engine displacement increase and the new silky smooth Turbo Hydramatic made the big Caddy an antelope among luxury car buffaloes. Automatic climate control, automatic headlights, rear-window defogger, and other power accessories pampered passengers and won converts. Although the Eldorado had long since been a special limited-production model, it was finally moved into the prestigious Fleetwood series that included the 60 Special, Series 75, and the jumbo block-long limousine. While the sporty Eldorado made no attempt at becoming a racing car, its 340-horsepower and rakish lines and sporty lack of rear-fender skirts promised sparkling touring back and forth to the country club. Sales still climbed.

1964 in Miniature

Faller of Germany made a bright pink 2½" plastic-bodied electric slot car of a 1964 Cadillac convertible for use on its HO slot-car track. Bumpers were plated, and two tiny but plump passengers occupied the flat interior. When other manufacturers were concentrating on slot car racers such as Corvettes and Mustangs, Faller was the only company willing to put the grand style back into mini grand touring.

Ideal Toys (USA/Hong Kong) created a line of plastic model car and truck bodies intended for use with a common interchangeable "Motorific" chassis, with twin AA batteries and a tiny electric motor. The cars or trucks would then putter around under their own power on the playroom floor or follow a slot in a snap-together plastic track through devilish obstacles. The idea was interesting, but its execution left much to be desired. The

Left to right: *Battery-powered 1964 Coupe de Villes in plastic by Ideal and die-cast by Mini-Dinky (note opening decks); 1964 S & S ambulance, Matchbox die-cast; and 1963 Series 62 convertible as HO slot car in plastic by Faller*

Jo-Han's plastic kit and plastic promo model of the 1964 Coupe de Ville

Motorific chassis, while rugged and inexpensive, was limited to one wheelbase. Since the car and truck bodies had to be stretched or shrunk to fit the chassis, scales varied wildly, and details were fudged. However, the 4½" Motorific 1964 Cadillac Coupe de Ville was one of the better efforts, with clear-plastic windows and plated bumpers, side trim, and fender trim.

Jo-Han made 1/25-scale plastic promotional/friction models and kits of the Coupe de Ville and de Ville convertible. The kits were molded in nonwarping polystyrene while the promotional and friction models were molded in glossy Cycolac plastic that resisted warp better than acetate. In addition, Jo-Han has reissued the 1964 de Ville convertible kit, and it is currently available at a fraction of the price of the original issue.

Matchbox of England made a 2⅞" die-cast metal Red Cross Cadillac ambulance. Bumpers were molded into the body and were painted silver. Windows and interior were plastic.

Mini-Dinky (Hong Kong) made a tiny 1/65-scale silver Coupe de Ville in die-cast metal. Despite its size, both hood and trunk opened. Proportions were excellent, and the shipping box was a tiny plastic garage with transparent walls. Unfortunately, many Mini-Dinky

Cadillacs become victims of fatal metal fatigue, and their bodies fall to pieces. Examine any Mini-Dinky Cadillac carefully before purchase.

Remarkably, still another cousin to the wonderfully weird gold(?)-plated 1961 and 1963 Cadillac cigarette case and lighter sets by Windsor is a 1964 Series 62 four-door sedan. Again, the trunk has an enormous lighter sticking up through it. Apparently this was the last model in this series of "executive gifts."

1964

Faller (Germany) 4857: Series 62 convertible, 2½", plastic; pink; obsolete; rare. Electric slot car. **$30 – 60**

Ideal (USA/Hong Kong): Series 62 Coupe de Ville, 4½", plastic; obsolete; rare. Body snapped onto standard battery-powered Motorific chassis. **$8 – 20**

Jo-Han (USA): Coupe de Ville, 1⁄25, plastic promo; obsolete; rare. **$45 – 75**

Jo-Han (USA): Coupe de Ville, 1⁄25, plastic kit; obsolete; rare. Original issue. **$8 – 45**

Jo-Han (USA) C-3764: Coupe de Ville, 1⁄25, plastic kit; current; common. Reissue of Windsor item. **$3 – 10**

Jo-Han (USA): de Ville convertible, 1⁄25, plastic promo; obsolete; rare. **$45 – 100**

Jo-Han (USA): de Ville convertible, 1⁄25, plastic kit; obsolete; rare. Original issue. **$8 – 45**

Jo-Han (USA) C-3964: de Ville convertible, 1⁄25, plastic kit, unpainted; current; common. Reissue. **$3 – 10**

Matchbox (GB) 54: S and S Cadillac ambulance, 2⅞", die-cast; white; obsolete; less common. Red Cross decal on doors. **$8 – 35**

Mini-Dinky (Hong Kong) 20: Coupe de Ville, 1⁄65, die-cast; silver; obsolete; rare. Opening hood and trunk; plastic garage shipping box. **$8 – 35**

Windsor (Japan): Series 62 four-door sedan, 8⅝", pot metal; gold-plated; obsolete; rare. Cigarette case with lighter. **$40 – 100**

1965

The Automobile

All-new styling marked 1965, and the tail fin dwindled further to a mere crease in the rear fender top. With the passing of the infamous tail fin, a styling era quietly ended. The Calais series replaced the Series 62 line in 1965. The pricier de Ville cars were equipped with plusher interiors and additional trim. The 60 Special received its own longer wheelbase and an optional Fleetwood Brougham trim package that included a padded roof. The Series 75 limousine still used the 1964 body that carried over the use of the huge wraparound windshield from earlier years — an updated body was still in the future.

1965 in Miniature

Asahi Toy Company of Japan made a 17" tin Coupe de Ville with friction power. Its window area and roof were rather tall, but the body captured the new slab-sided 1965 styling very well. Surely the lack of complex body curves made steel stampings easier to manufacture. Interestingly, the box depicted a sedan with 1966 trim.

From Bandai of Japan came an 8" tin Sedan de Ville that had a shallow lithographed interior with a plastic steering wheel.

Ichiko of Japan made a 22" two-tone tin 1965 Calais with friction drive. This was a four-door sedan with center posts and not a hardtop sedan.

Jo-Han made de Ville hardtop and convertible plastic promotional models and kits again. The model kits featured opening hoods and model engines, whereas the promotional models did not. Sharp collectors also note that the kit interiors are more accurately detailed.

Sakura of Japan made a striking 1⁄43-scale die-cast Fleetwood Brougham (actually a 60 Special since it lacked the padded Brougham roof treatment) that seemed as heavy as a brick. The windows were darkly tinted in blue and concealed the lack of interior detail. The plated body was painted in the style reminiscent of the Banthrico and National Products models of years past; the trim and window surrounds were masked, and the body was then sprayed with gloss black, leaving the silver masked body trim to shine through when the masks were removed. Packed in a flocked red display box, Sakura created an impressive die-cast Caddy that has a strange visual likeness to a scaled-down Japanese tin toy.

1965

Asahi (Japan): Coupe de Ville, 17", "tin"; red; obsolete; rarest. Friction. **$150 – 500**

Bandai (Japan): Sedan de Ville, 8", tin, obsolete, rare. **$100 – 150**

Sakura's die-cast 1965 Fleetwood Brougham sedan

Note the lithographed interior in this 8" tin Sedan de Ville by Bandai

Ichiko (Japan): Calais (replaces 62 sedan), 22", "tin"; red; obsolete; rarest. Friction. **$200 – 525**

Jo-Han (USA): Coupe de Ville, 1⁄25, plastic promo; obsolete; rare. **$35 – 100**

Jo-Han (USA) C1765: Coupe de Ville, 1⁄25, plastic kit; obsolete; rare. **$15 – 60**

Jo-Han (USA): de Ville convertible, 1⁄25, plastic promo; obsolete; rare. **$35 – 125**

Jo-Han (USA) C1765: de Ville convertible, plastic kit, unpainted; obsolete; rare. **$15 – 65**

Sakura (Japan) A-3: Fleetwood Brougham sedan, 1⁄43, die-cast; black; rare. Actually a 60 Special. **$35 – 100**

1966

The Automobile

The elegant understated restyling of 1965 was only mildly changed for 1966. Stylists' continued restrained use of chrome reinforced a new conservative Brooks Brothers image at Cadillac. Efforts were concentrated on improving passenger comfort, including a new stereo sound system, variable-ratio power steering, and elaborate sound deadening. The Fleetwood Series 75 finally received updated styling and engineering in 1966, and the panoramic wraparound windshield of the limousine body went the way of the tall tail fin into auto oblivion.

1966 in Miniature

Dinky Toys of England made a 6" Superior Rescue Ambulance in die-cast metal. The rear hatch opened to reveal a tiny patient on a plastic stretcher. Quality was not a high priority on this model; both fit and red and white finish suffered somewhat. In addition, the front fenders carried incorrect 1965-style cornering lights. Early versions were numbered #262 while later "Speedwheel" versions were numbered #288. A special FALCK ambulance was produced for the Danish market only.

Jo-Han created a veritable herd of plastic 1⁄25-scale Cadillacs for 1966. In addition to promotional and kit models of the de Ville coupe and convertible, Jo-Han also offered a detailed kit of a 1966 Superior ambulance as well as a hearse with casket. A later and more light-hearted reissue was dubbed the "Heavenly Hearse" (still # GC-600) and equipped with surfboards! There was even a "Roaring Rambulance Drag Car." The kits all included opening hoods and model engines.

Japanese kitmaker Hasegawa currently offers a plastic 1⁄24-scale Coupe de Ville kit. The model is comparable to the Jo-Han in body and trim, but Hasegawa cut corners on the interior with a flat, generic dashboard with a decal for Cadillac instrumentation and trim. This dash is shared with several other American plastic car kits in this series. Such penny-wise but pound-foolish details keep this from being a really nice kit. In addition, the Hasegawa kit lacks an opening hood and a model engine.

Praline (Germany), under the Revell label, currently offers a plastic HO-scale Series 75 limousine in a variety of colors for the model-railroad trade. Additional variations

Foreground: *1966 Superior Rescue Ambulance, die-cast Dinky Toy with mixture of 1965 and 1966 trim, and '66 Fleetwood 75 limousine, die-cast by Siku, with jeweled headlights and opening doors — a rare model in an odd 1/55 scale (Ferd Zegel Collection).* ***Behind:*** *Jo-Han's 1966 Fire Rescue Ambulance kit, in plastic, and '66 Heavenly Hearse kit, plastic, which could be built as either stock hearse or "surf-party machine"!*

Left to right: *Hasegawa kit for plastic 1966 Coupe de Ville, '66 convertible as plastic promo by Jo-Han, and Jo-Han's kit for Coupe de Ville, in plastic*

include a limousine with American flags on fender masts and even a Texas tycoon version with hood-mounted steerhorns and silkscreened American flag on the roof! Other special-body Praline 1966 Cadillacs include an ambulance and a hearse.

Siku of Germany offered a 1⁄55-scale die-cast Series 75 limousine with opening doors and tiny jeweled headlights. The candy red paint job left much to be desired, and the body was too squat and wide.

1966

Dinky Toys (GB) 262 and 288: Superior Rescue Ambulance, 6", die-cast; red/white; obsolete; rare. Actually has 1965 cornering lights on front fenders. **$30 – 60**

Hasegawa (Japan) CB1: Coupe de Ville, 1⁄24, plastic kit, unpainted; current; common. **$7 – 20**

Jo-Han (USA): Coupe de Ville, 1⁄25, plastic promo; obsolete; rare. **$35 – 90**

Jo-Han (USA) C1366: Coupe de Ville, 1⁄25, plastic kit, unpainted; obsolete; rare. **$15 – 50**

Jo-Han (USA): de Ville convertible, 1⁄25, plastic promo; obsolete; rare. **$35 – 125**

Jo-Han (USA): de Ville convertible, 1⁄25, plastic kit, unpainted; obsolete; rare. **$15 – 80**

Jo-Han (USA) GC-500: ambulance, 1⁄25, plastic kit, unpainted; current; common. **$5 – 10**

Jo-Han (USA) GC-600: "Heavenly Hearse," 1⁄25, plastic kit, unpainted; current; common. Variation on ambulance body. **$5 – 10**

Jo-Han (USA) 800: "Roaring Rambulance Drag Car," 1⁄25, plastic kit, unpainted; obsolete; less common. Variation on the ambulance kit, above. **$5 – 25**

Praline (Germany): ambulance, HO, plastic; current; common. Hearse variation also available. **$3 – 6**

Praline (Germany): Fleetwood Series 75 limousine, HO, plastic; current; common. Interesting variations include U.S. fender flags and even steerhorn hood ornament. **$3 – 6**

Siku (Germany): Fleetwood Series 75 limousine, 1⁄55, die-cast; red; obsolete; rare. Jeweled headlights. **$20 – 90**

Parked ***(left to right)*** *are Praline models of 1966 hearse, ambulance variations, diplomatic limousine with fender flags, a standard limousine, and a Texas version.*

1967

The Automobile

The Fleetwood Eldorado of 1967 was the finest Eldorado yet. Bill Mitchell's GM styling staff created the first new Eldorado that was more than a specially bodied show car or a modified Series 62 body, although a convertible Eldorado would not be offered again for several years. Sharing the front-wheel drive platform developed for the fabulous new Oldsmobile Toronado, it was the right car for the right time. The Eldorado's sleek lines appealed to affluent young professionals as well as to the older traditional Cadillac clientele. Car buyers who never considered a Cadillac purchase before were buying Eldorados. Fine handling and classic design earned praise and even the *Automobile Quarterly* Design and Engineering Award.

The conventional rear-wheel drive Cadillacs for 1967 continued the understated minimal-chrome trim approach that had worked so successfully in recent styling. Body sculpturing was redrawn, but it reinforced traditional Cadillac panache.

1967 in Miniature

Bandai of Japan made a 13" tin toy of the revolutionary new 1967 Eldorado. This toy was equipped with a battery-powered electric motor and non-Cadillac-style mag wheels that would be more appropriate to a dragster.

Husky Models of England made a 3" die-cast Eldorado with opening hood, plastic windows, and interior. Later, Husky toys were reissued as Corgi Juniors and equipped

Collection of 1967 Eldorado coupes. ***Top:*** *Die-cast Dinky Toys, with opening hood, doors, and trunk (Ferd Zegel Collection).* ***Middle:*** *Sabra/Cragstan die-casts; note Israeli government markings on dark blue car (Ferd Zegel Collection).* ***Bottom:*** *Die-cast Husky, die-cast Corgi with "Whizzwheels," die-cast Lone Star Flyer with snap-on roof rack with four spare tires.*

Jo-Han's plastic promos of the 1967 de Ville convertible and the Eldorado coupe, in front of Jo-Han's kit for the Eldorado coupe

Opening doors, hood, and trunk as well as an electric motor are features of this Schuco plastic and metal 1967 de Ville convertible.

with ugly black "Whizzwheels" to compete with Mattel's successful "Hot Wheels" series of lightning-fast, pocket-sized, die-cast toy cars.

Lone Star Flyer (England) made a poorly cast and finished 3" 1967 Eldorado that could have been copied from the Husky/ Corgi Junior toy. The opening hood was eliminated, and a strange vinyl plastic roof rack with four spare tires covered the entire roof. Talk about pessimists!

Dinky of England die-cast a 5⅛" Eldorado with opening hood, doors, and trunk. One issue of this model was painted purple with yellow interior! Dinky Toy quality was clearly on the slide (and color-blind).

Ichiko of Japan made a huge 22" tin Eldorado with friction power. This model is now highly prized and commands high dollar for a mint example. Unfortunately, the bigger the tin toy, the more likely it was to be abused, for it was tempting for youngsters to sit on it, ride it, and thus dent it badly.

Jo-Han made 1⁄25-scale promotional models and kits of the 1967 de Ville hardtop and convertible. In addition, Jo-Han also made a 1⁄25-scale promotional model and kit of the new Eldorado coupe. The promotional models lacked the opening hoods and model engines that the kits featured.

Miller Memorabilia offered a handcast 1⁄25-scale resin model of the Eldorado made to individual order.

Processed Plastics made a 1⁄20 Eldorado in vinyl plastic with flash-plated bumpers and even clear windows. The stock version is rather nice, if pudgy. However, a later "street racer" version boggles the mind with chromed velocity stacks bulging from a large hood cut-out and huge drag slicks mounted on the jacked-up *rear* axle. The folks at Processed Plastics apparently forgot that one of the 1967 Eldo's greatest claims to fame was its wonderful front-wheel drive system.

Sabra of Israel created a die-cast series of 1⁄43 American cars and trucks of the 1960s and marketed them through Cragstan Toys in the United States. Each car came packaged in a handy flat-roofed clear plastic garage with a swing-up vinyl plastic garage door. One of the better automotive issues was the 1967 Eldorado. The body lines are captured well, but the interior is bloblike. An unusual version of this particular Eldo is an Israeli goverment staff car imprinted with government crests on the doors!

Schuco of Germany made one of the most interesting 1967 Cadillac de Ville convertible model/toys in 1⁄20 scale. Bumpers and chassis were metal while the body was plastic. The hood opened to expose a flashy, chromed, dummy engine. The opening trunk revealed the battery box for two AA penlight batteries that powered an electric motor. The doors opened to reveal the most interesting feature of all — lighted green, red, and yellow buttons between the front bucket seats that controlled forward, stop, and reverse action. A young Cadillac enthusiast could crank the steerable front wheels into position and punch the appropriate button to power the sleek convertible across the playroom with a minimum of fuss. How like Dad's car!

Nutz (Germany) currently reissues the 1⁄20-scale motorized Schuco Cadillac convertible complete with push-button drive. The Nutz knock-off copy lacks the plated hubcaps of the Schuco car and the fender skirts. Inexplicably, some of the Nutz cars are decorated with decals of daisies! Flower Power?

1967

Aurora (USA) 50-367: Coupe de Ville, 1⁄32, plastic kit, unpainted; obsolete; less common. **$10 – 25**

Bandai (Japan): Eldorado hardtop, 13", "tin"; blue; obsolete; rare. Battery; odd mag-style hubcaps. **$35 – 90**

Corgi Junior Whizzwheels (GB): Eldorado hardtop, 3", die-cast; metallic green/red interior; obsolete; less common. Same car as Husky, below, but with Whizzwheels. **$5 – 10**

Processed Plastics' 1967 Eldorado street racer

Dinky Toys (GB) 175: Eldorado hardtop, 1⁄43, die-cast; purple or blue; obsolete; less common. Crude and heavy; opening doors, hood, trunk. **$20 – 75**

Husky (GB): Eldorado hardtop, 3", die-cast; blue/red interior; obsolete; less common. Opening hood, chrome wheels with separate tires, trailer hitch. **$5 – 10**

Ichiko (Japan): Eldorado hardtop, 22", "tin"; red; obsolete; rarest. Huge. Friction. **$250 – 800**

Jo-Han (USA): Coupe de Ville, 1⁄25, plastic promo; obsolete; rare. **$30 – 90**

Jo-Han (USA): Coupe de Ville, 1⁄25, plastic kit, unpainted; obsolete; rare. **$10 – 50**

Jo-Han (USA): de Ville convertible, 1⁄25, plastic promo; obsolete; rare. **$35 – 100**

Jo-Han (USA): de ville convertible, 1⁄25, plastic kit, unpainted; obsolete; rare. **$10 – 50**

Jo-Han (USA): Eldorado hardtop, 1⁄25, plastic promo; obsolete; rare. **$35 – 70**

Jo-Han (USA) C1867: Eldorado hardtop, 1⁄25, plastic kit, unpainted; obsolete; rare. **$10 – 50**

Lone Star Flyer (GB): Eldorado hardtop, 1⁄87, die-cast; red; obsolete; rare. Copy of Husky/Corgi; odd clip-on roof rack with four spare tires. **$5 – 8**

Miller Memorabilia (USA) CC138: Eldorado hardtop, 1⁄25, resin kit, unpainted; obsolete; less common. **$20 -40**

Nutz (Germany) 5505: de Ville convertible, 1⁄20, plastic; current; common. Reissue of Schuco #5505; no fender skirts or plated hubcaps. **$20 – 50**

Processed Plastic (USA): Eldorado coupe, 1⁄20; vinyl plastic; blue; obsolete; rare. Variations include an odd hot rod version. **$10 – 40**

Sabra (Israel) 8110: Eldorado hardtop, 1⁄43, die-cast; obsolete; less common. Marketed by Cragstan (USA). **$10 – 35**

Schuco (Germany) 5505: de Ville convertible, 1⁄20, plastic/metal; red or silver; obsolete; rare. Electric motor; opening hood, doors, trunk; push button controls. **$45 – 100**

1968

The Automobile

The big Cadillac news of 1968 was the new monster 472-cid V-8 engine, the largest production passenger car engine in the world. Also in 1968, the three-millionth car rolled off the Cadillac assembly line. Styling changes on the bread-and-butter rear-drive Cadillacs were difficult to spot unless the 1967 and 1968 models were parked side by side. The grille shape was altered, the hood was changed, concealed windshield wipers were included, and government-mandated side-marker lights were added.

The Eldorado sported relocated parking lamps and concealed windshield wipers like those introduced on other Cadillacs. For reasons best known only to Cadillac, disk brakes remained an option.

1968 in Miniature

Bandai of Japan was a well-known producer of tin toys, but it was Bandai of Korea which made a 13⅓" tin 1968 convertible with four doors. One can only speculate that it was cut down from a sedan model/toy. Features included steerable front wheels, an electric motor, and even a horn. Great fun.

Jo-Han (USA) made plastic 1⁄25-scale promotional models and kits of the Coupe de Ville, de Ville convertible, and Eldorado. The promotional models lacked the kits' opening hoods and model engines. Ex-El products has dusted off the old Jo-Han dies and reissued the 1968 Coupe de Ville and de Ville convertible promotional models for those who missed them the first time around. These are bargains. Note the use of plastic pins instead of screws on the chassis of reproduction versions.

Gamda Koor Sabra of Israel produced a series of American cars in 1⁄43 scale that were crude but interesting. Distributed by Cragstan and packed in a clear plastic box that resembled a garage, each car usually had one opening feature — such as hood, trunk, or doors — but never more than one. The Sabra 1968 de Ville convertible captured the lines of the car, but the doors opened to reveal a perfectly awful bloblike vinyl-plastic interior. The Sabra 1968 de Ville convertible also had a snap-on plastic convertible roof and an opening trunk. The plated bumpers were fair, but showed lack of quality control in plating and assembly. These were always intended to be inexpensive and disposable toys.

An early Mattel Hot Wheels (USA) was a mildly customized 3" die-cast 1968 Eldorado. Aside from the hotrod hood with power bulges, the lakes pipes, and the

Top: Jo-Han's plastic promo 1968 Coupe de Ville and its kit for the plastic de Ville convertible; this was reissued as the "Boss Man" edition, presumably to capitalize on the popularity of Boss Hogg, proud owner of a white Cadillac convertible on TV's "The Dukes of Hazzard." ***Bottom:*** *Jo-Han's plastic promos of the '68 Eldorado coupe and the de Ville convertible.*

mag-style wheels with red-line tires, the tiny candy-colored Eldo is not bad for an inexpensive toy. In fact, Mattel even went the extra step to paint the roof flat black to simulate a vinyl roof. A mint example still on the bubble card with the collector button is a rapidly appreciating collectible.

1968

Bandai (Korea): four-door convertible, 13¼", "tin"; red; obsolete; rare. Sedan cut down into convertible; electric motor and horn, steering. **$35 – 100**

Jo-Han (USA): Coupe de Ville, 1⁄25, plastic promo; obsolete; rare. Original issue. **$10 – 60**

Jo-Han/Ex-El (USA): Coupe de Ville, 1⁄25, plastic promo; current; common. Ex-El promo reissue. **$10 – 40**

Jo-Han (USA): Coupe de Ville, 1⁄25, plastic kit, unpainted; obsolete; rare. **$10 – 45**

Jo-Han (USA): de Ville convertible, 1⁄25, plastic promo; obsolete; rare. **$25 – 80**

Jo-Han/Ex-El (USA): de Ville convertible, 1⁄25, plastic promo; current; common. Ex-El promo reissue. **$10 – 40**

Jo-Han (USA): de Ville convertible, 1⁄25, plastic kit, unpainted; obsolete; rare. **$10 – 55**

Jo-Han (USA) C5368: de Ville convertible, 1⁄25, plastic kit; current; common. Kit reissue. **$4 – 10**

Jo-Han (USA): Eldorado hardtop, 1⁄25, plastic promo; obsolete; rare. **$35 – 75**

Jo-Han (USA): Eldorado hardtop, 1⁄25, plastic kit, unpainted; obsolete; rare. **$10 – 50**

1968 "Custom Eldorados," die-cast by Mattel Hot Wheels (note early series "red-line" tires); '68 de Ville convertible die-cast by Sabra/Cragstan

Bandai's pressed-steel 1968 four-door convertible includes electric horn and motor as well as working steering wheel.

Mattel Hot Wheels (USA): Custom Eldorado hardtop, 3", die-cast; obsolete; rare when in original packaging. Red-line speed wheels, opening hood, flat black top, lakes pipes. **$3 – 35**

Sabra (Israel) 8123: de Ville convertible, 1/43, die-cast; obsolete; less common. Removable convertible top and opening trunk. Distributed by Cragstan. **$10 – 35**

1969

The Automobile

Labor problems held Cadillac production back in 1969, and total sales were down almost seven thousand cars from 1968. Nonetheless, it was still a good year. The Eldorado, with new grille and exposed headlights, found itself pitted against the new Thunderbird-based Lincoln Continental Mark III. The de Villes received new front-end styling with horizontal headlights and just a hint of high rear-fender line that vaguely suggested the glory days of the tail fin. Disk brakes were *finally* made standard equipment.

Jo-Han's plastic promos of the 1969 Coupe de Ville and Eldorado coupe, in front of Jo-Han's kits for these two cars

1969 in Miniature

Ertl (USA) made an inexpensive 3⅛" die-cast de Ville convertible decorated as TV's *The Dukes of Hazzard*'s Boss Hogg Cadillac complete with steerhorn hood ornament and the Boss's name silkscreened on the fender. Some examples had stickers rather than silkcreening. Bizarre Americana!

An unknown Canadian toy manufacturer made a crude 1/20-scale plastic toy of Boss Hogg's 1969 Cadillac big enough for a chubby little action figure of Boss to drive. Why didn't the good guys get to drive the Caddy?

Jo-Han again offered plastic 1/25-scale promotional models and kits of the Coupe de Ville and Eldorado. The promotional models came prepainted in authentic colors and lacked the kits' opening hoods and model engines. For unknown reasons, the de Ville convertible was not offered as a promotional or a kit in 1969. A loss!

1969

Ertl (USA): de Ville convertible, 3⅛", die-cast; white; obsolete; common. *The Dukes of Hazzard* car; silkscreened or sticker of "Boss Hogg" on fender; steerhorn hood ornament. **$.50 – 5**

Jo-Han (USA): Coupe de Ville, 1/25, plastic promo; obsolete; less common. **$35 – 65**

Jo-Han (USA) C1769: Coupe de Ville, 1/25, plastic kit, unpainted; obsolete; less common. **$25 – 55**

Jo-Han (USA): Eldorado hardtop, 1/25, plastic promo; obsolete; less common. **$25 – 65**

Jo-Han (USA) C1269: Eldorado hardtop, 1/25, plastic kit, unpainted; obsolete; less common. **$10 – 35**

Unknown (Canada): de Ville convertible, 1/20, vinyl plastic; white; obsolete; rare. *The Dukes of Hazzard* car with TV action figure. **$10 – 75**

1970

The Automobile

The 1970 Eldorado broke new ground with a standard 400-horsepower engine displacing a whopping 500 cubic inches, the largest production V-8 in the world. All 1970 models were mildly face-lifted for the last time in the cycle before the debut of the new 1971 models. The lower-priced Calais series continued to try to tempt entry-level Cadillac buyers, but sales were only lukewarm. The de Ville convertible made its farewell

Jo-Han plastic promo of 1970 Eldorado coupe, with Jo-Han's kit for the same model

1970 de Ville convertibles: Ertl's die-cast Boss Hogg car and a die-cast (manufacturer unknown) with many odd graphics, presumed to be crude copies of the Ertl model

1970 Coupe de Ville, from resin kit by Hessmania, a limited edition to commemorate the travels of famed postcard photographer James Hess, and two die-cast Eldorado coupes, manufacturer unknown

appearance in 1970, for the new 1971 Eldorado convertible was destined to become the only Cadillac ragtop in the new styling cycle.

1970 in Miniature

Miller Memorabilia made a tiny 1/87-scale 1970 Coupe de Ville under a special "Hessmania" label that commemorated the travels of a postcard photographer named Hess, who made his living traveling throughout the eastern states photographing diners and motels. He never failed to include his own personal Cadillac in his postcard pictures. Now that was brand loyalty!

Jo-Han made 1/25-scale promotional and kit models of the Coupe de Ville and Eldorado. The promotional models were pre-assembled and painted, lacking the kits' opening hoods and model engines.

An unknown Hong Kong company produced a tiny 2¾" 1970 Eldorado coupe with incorrect rectangular head lamps, nasty imitation Hot Wheels, and "Eldorato" imprinted on the chassis.

1970

Hessmania (USA) 2: Coupe de Ville, 1/87, resin; metallic blue; obsolete; rare. Cottage industry. **$5 – 15**

Jo-Han (USA): Coupe de Ville, 1/25, plastic promo; obsolete; less common. **$20 – 60**

Jo-Han (USA): Coupe de Ville, 1/25, plastic kit, unpainted; obsolete; less common. **$20 – 60**

Jo-Han (USA): Eldorado hardtop, 1/25, plastic promo; obsolete; less common. **$20 – 60**

Jo-Han (USA): Eldorado hardtop, 1/25, plastic kit, unpainted; current reissue; common. **$3 – 10**

Unknown (Hong Kong): Eldorado hardtop, 2¾", die-cast; obsolete; less common. "Eldorato" (sic) on chassis; crude, wrong rectangular head lamps. **$1 – 2**

1971

The Automobile

The first completely new Cadillacs since 1961 were immediate hits. For the first time Cadillacs were built in two different cities, with the addition of a New Jersey assembly plant. All Cadillacs were detuned to operate on regular 91-octane unleaded gasoline; as a result, horsepower dropped. The Eldorado outsold the Continental Mark III by less than three hundred cars, despite the Eldo's availability as both a coupe or new convertible compared to the Continental's availability as only a two-door coupe. A new smaller Cadillac was on the drawing board.

1971 in Miniature

The only 1971 Cadillac toys and models were Eldorados. The rest of the line seems to have been ignored. Toy- and modelmakers of the era concentrated on sportier

AMR's die-cast of the 1971 Eldorado convertible

Top:** 1971 Eldorados: AMR die-cast convertible and Mini-Lindy plastic snap kits of the coupe, with Britains gasoline pump.* ***Bottom: *Jo-Han plastic promos of 1971 and 1972 Eldorado coupe.*

cars such as the Mustang, Camaro, and Firebird. Perhaps, too, American values had changed for the members of the younger generation, and Cadillac was not the symbol of success it had been to their parents.

In the late 1980s AMR of France made a gorgeous 1⁄43-scale model of the 1971 Eldorado convertible in white metal. Available in a kit or factory assembled and painted, this model was perfect. Photo-etched trim and decaled details made this a breathtaking miniature, and despite its small scale, still a heavy model to hold in one hand. A less common (and even more expensive) variation was an Eldorado coupe.

Jo-Han built a 1971 Eldorado coupe promotional model and kit. The kit had an opening hood and a model engine. The promo model did not.

Finally, Lindberg models made a tiny 1⁄64-scale 1971 Eldorado coupe in a series called "Mini-Lindys." These models came molded in colors with plated bumpers, and they snapped together easily. Two screws held the chassis in place. The last re-release of this mini-Eldorado in the mid-1980s even included a plastic model garage!

1971

AMR (France): Eldorado coupe, 1⁄43, die-cast; obsolete; less common. Expensive handbuilt. **$100 – 250**

AMR (France) 484: Eldorado convertible, 1⁄43, die-cast; obsolete; less common. Expensive handbuilt. **$75 – 175**

Jo-Han (USA): Eldorado hardtop, 1⁄25, plastic promo; obsolete; less common. **$20 – 60**

Jo-Han (USA): Eldorado hardtop, 1⁄25, plastic kit, unpainted; obsolete; less common. **$10 – 35**

Lindberg (USA) D-230: Eldorado coupe, 1⁄64, plastic kit; obsolete; less common. Simple plastic kit. **$2 – 5**

1972

The Automobile

The seventieth anniversary edition of Cadillac was largely a face-lift of the recently restyled 1971 version. Minor mechanical changes improved drivability in the face of new tougher emissions regulations, and an anti-skid braking system was an available option across the board. The Eldorado was the only model to be powered by the King Kong 500-cid engine. For the first time, the Continental Mark IV outsold the Eldorado. Distinguishing the new 1972 Cadillacs outwardly was the relocation of the flow-through ventilation louvers from the trunk lid to the door posts.

1972 in Miniature

Jo-Han built the only 1972 Cadillac model, an Eldorado coupe. A promotional model and a kit version were available. The kit featured an opening hood and a model

Top: Plastic model kit of 1973 Eldorado "Rancher" from Jo-Han; note that while the picture on the box is a '73 car, Jo-Han has been known to substitute other year models. ***Below:*** *1973 Eldorado convertible Indianapolis 500 pace car in plastic by Jo-Han, a "kit chop" of the coupe model with the fine Fred Cady aftermarket decals; Jo-Han plastic promo of the coupe.*

engine; the promotional model did not. Model- and toymakers were concentrating their efforts on sports and muscle cars, for they were youngsters' new dream cars.

1972

Jo-Han (USA): Eldorado hardtop, 1⁄25, plastic promo; obsolete; less common. **$20 – 45**

Jo-Han (USA): Eldorado hardtop, 1⁄25, plastic kit, unpainted; obsolete; less common. **$8 – 35**

1973

The Automobile

Cadillac returned to Indianapolis to pace the 500-mile Memorial Day Classic for a fifth time with a sleek, white Eldorado convertible in 1973. Jim Rathmann, the 1960 Indy winner, was at the wheel. Up to that time, the only other front-drive Indy pace car had been the rakish coffin-nosed 1930 Cord.

Massive, government-mandated, impact-absorbing bumpers were added to all Cadillacs. The Continental Mark IV handily outsold the Eldorado, but the de Ville series outsold the standard Lincoln by more than three to one. The Arab oil embargo and its destabilizing effects on the auto market hastened work on a smaller Cadillac, and Americans rethought their big car habit as they endured long gas lines. The times they were a-changin'.

1973 in Miniature

There were only two 1973 Cadillac scale models, both 1/25-scale Eldorados, and both done by Jo-Han. The first was a factory-assembled and painted promotional model, and the second was a kit with opening hood and model engine. An ambitious modeler could duplicate the Indy Eldo by removing the Jo-Han model's roof and adding Fred Cady aftermarket Indy pace car decals!

The remainder of the line was once again ignored by toy- and modelmakers who had discovered that Mercedes and Porsche toys and models sold well.

1973

Jo-Han (USA): Eldorado hardtop, 1/25, plastic promo; obsolete, less common. **$20 – 35**

Jo-Han (USA): Eldorado hardtop, 1/25, plastic kit, unpainted; obsolete; less common. **$8 – 20**

Jo-Han (USA) GC-3300: Eldorado "Rancher" hardtop, 1/25, plastic kit, unpainted; current; less common. Texas "Rancher" decals on a stock kit. *Note*: Jo-Han often substitutes other year Eldorados in the "Rancher," despite the picture on the box. **$4 – 10**

1974

The Automobile

The turmoil of the Arab oil embargo and the resulting shortages hurt sales of all big cars, and Cadillac built over 20 percent fewer cars in 1974. Gas lines sent American motorists scurrying to buy smaller cars that delivered high gas mileage. Foreign makers offered the right products at the right time and greatly increased their market share. While Cadillac stressed that its cars delivered fuel-efficient performance, the days of the big block/big body Cadillac were numbered until new cars could be designed to meet the challenge of a new automotive era. Changes for 1974 centered on improving durability and comfort. One notable Cadillac styling change was the disappearance of the true hardtop; a coupe with fixed rear quarter windows replaced it.

The Continental Mark IV coupe still outsold the Eldorado coupe and convertible, but the standard Cadillac line proved more popular than the standard uninspired Lincoln offerings for 1974. Chrysler's Imperial was a dismal shadow of its former self and would be axed in an

Top: *1974 and 1975 Eldorado coupes, Jo-Han plastic promos.* ***Bottom:*** *Resin kit from Miller Memorabilia of 1975 Seville.*

inevitable product line reshuffling; it would be a mercy killing.

Cadillac still had an ace up its corporate sleeve for 1975 — the new Mercedes-sized Seville.

1974 in Miniature

Jo-Han proved again to be the only model manufacturer to carry the Cadillac name for 1974. A 1974 Eldorado promotional model and a kit were the only new Cadillac miniatures available. The promotional model was factory assembled and painted and did not share the kit's opening hood and model engine. Automotive tastes were changing — even among modelmakers and toymakers.

1974

Jo-Han (USA): Eldorado hardtop, 1/25, plastic promo; obsolete; less common. **$10 – 35**

Jo-Han (USA): Eldorado hardtop, 1/25, plastic kit, unpainted; obsolete; less common. **$8 – 15**

1975

The Automobile

The debut of the Seville was the high point of Cadillac's 1975 model year. After suffering criticism for safety-related engineering problems and poor quality control, Cadillac management took special pains to guarantee Seville assembly met the highest standards. As a result, the new Seville proved a success.

The Continental Mark IV still outsold the restyled Eldorado by a thin margin, but the 1975 Eldorado showed that a larger car could also be a graceful and lovely design. With new rectangular head lamps (standard on all Cadillacs), new grille, and lack of fender skirts, the 500-cid Eldorado was a strikingly elegant luxury car that turned heads and pampered its passengers.

1975 in Miniature

Jo-Han faithfully updated its molds for a plastic 1/25-scale Eldorado promotional and kit model as in years past. The promotional again came painted and assembled and did not share the opening hood feature with the model kit.

A 1/35-scale 1975 Seville was offered by Miller Memorabilia as a resin kit. The windows were opaque, the model lacked an interior, and the wheels were separate and could be made to turn. Detail fidelity was good.

Tom Mills' TKM Models made a 1/25-scale resin kit of the new Seville. Windows were opaque and cast with the body. There was no interior, and (like the Miller model) bumpers and hubcaps were not plated. Although TKM models required some modeling skill for smooth finishing, the TKM Seville was a good companion piece to the Jo-Han models.

1975

Jo-Han (USA): Eldorado hardtop, 1/25, plastic promo; obsolete; less common. **$8 – 25**

Jo-Han (USA): Eldorado hardtop, 1/25, plastic kit, unpainted; obsolete; less common. **$6 – 15**

Miller Memorabilia (USA) 3501: Seville, 1/35, resin kit, unpainted; obsolete; less common. **$12 – 30**

TKM (USA): Seville, 1/25, resin kit, unpainted; obsolete; less common. **$15 – 35**

1976

The Automobile

Styling and engineering changes were few in 1976, in anticipation of a major makeover of the standard full-sized de Ville scheduled for 1977. Sales in 1975 had increased while industry sales as a whole were down. The new Seville was attracting potential foreign car buyers as planned, and the General was pleased. Government involvement in dictating car design spelled the end of the convertible, and the 1976 Eldorado was billed as the last of the great Cadillac convertibles. This would eventually prove to be a premature epitaph, for the Cadillac

***Top:** Built and unbuilt Jo-Han plastic snap-kit 1976 Eldorado coupe. **Bottom:** Kit chop to modify snap-kit coupe into a 1976 Eldorado.*

convertible would be reborn in 1984. Nevertheless, at the time, Cadillac touted the last two hundred specially painted white Eldorado convertibles as immediate collectibles. As oil availability and prices stabilized again, demand for big cars would increase. The Continental outsold Eldorado by a small margin, although the standard Cadillac range outsold Lincoln again. It was a fickle marketplace, and decisions made at the height of the oil crisis would have long-reaching effects.

1976 in Miniature

With renewed optimism for the future marketplace, model- and toymakers seemed more willing to commit themselves to making more models of luxury cars such as Cadillacs.

An unknown manufacturer made a 1/35-scale pewter 1976 Seville promotional(?) model mounted on a sculptured base. Reminiscent of the automotive castings of National Products, it had opaque windows and wheels that did not turn. It weighed in at a porky 4½ pounds and originally came in its own plush presentation case. At better than a hundred 1976 dollars, this was a capital investment in pewter, much less in models. It is rumored that only a thousand were made.

Jo-Han made a 1/25-scale plastic promotional model of the 1976 Eldorado. The same mold was later used for a snap-together kit (that is still commonly available), and these kits are frequently confused for promotional models. The most common molded-plastic color for the snap-kit 1976 Eldorado is a bright blue. The promotional models were generally molded in white plastic, and then the bodies were painted in Cadillac colors while the interior and chassis remained unpainted white plastic.

Tomica Pocket Cars of Japan made a tiny 1/77-scale die-cast Fleetwood Brougham sedan. Tomica is known for getting the most out of a single casting by making several variations with different paint and trim. The

Tomica die-cast "Pocket Car" Series for 1976 line. ***Top:*** *Fleetwood Broughams, ambulance sedan, state trooper version of Fleetwood Brougham, and Superior Ambulance (chassis plate is same as sedan).* ***Bottom:*** *Three other color variations of Tomica's Fleetwood Brougham and Yatming's die-cast Fleetwood Broughams, presumed to be copies of Tomicas.*

Tomica Fleetwood Brougham came in solid and two-tone paint jobs as well as in police car and Red Cross liveries. To further confuse collectors, all variations used the same baseplate and number (F2). An additional Tomica 1976 Cadillac was a Superior Ambulance. This also used the same baseplate and number, but "Fleetwood Brougham" was blocked out. It was fitting that after years of being ignored by toymakers, the de Ville was again done in miniature.

Yatming (Hong Kong) copied the Tomica Fleetwood Brougham in red. A further Chinese-built Yatming sported strange red, white, and blue Cadillac crest graphics.

In 1991 Elegance of France produced a 1/43-scale 1976 Cadillac Fleetwood Brougham and a custom stretch landau version. These were hand-assembled museum quality models of great detail. However, they were also *very* expensive and difficult to find.

1976

Elegance (France) 153: Fleetwood Brougham, 1/43, resin; current; less common. Factory-built limited edition. **$200 – 450**

Elegance (France) 146b: landau stretch limousine, 1/43, resin; current; less common. Factory-built limited edition. **$200 – 450**

Jo-Han (USA): Eldorado hardtop, 1/25, plastic promo; obsolete; less common. Some old stock still available through Ex-El. **$8 – 20**

Jo-Han (USA) CS-501: Eldorado hardtop, 1/25, plastic kit; blue; current; common. Snap-together kit; looks like an unassembled promo model. **$3 – 7**

Nolatoy (USA) 4011: Eldorado convertible, 1/20, plastic toy; obsolete; less common. Battery-powered electric drive. **$30 – 75**

Tomica Pocket Cars (Japan) F2: Fleetwood Brougham, 1/77, die-cast; current; less common. Also available in Red Cross and police liveries. **$3 – 10**

Tomica Pocket Cars (Japan) F2: Superior Ambulance, 1/77, die-cast; red/white top; current; less common. Same Serial # as Fleetwood Brougham, above; chassis has other model name blocked out. **$3 – 10**

Unknown: Seville, 1/35, pewter promo; obsolete; rare. Mounted on base; 4½ lbs. **$50 – 125**

Yatming (Hong Kong, China built) 1053: Fleetwood Brougham, 1/77, die-cast; metallic red; current; less common. Copy of Tomica F2; Chinese version has garish red/white/blue graphics. **$1 – 3**

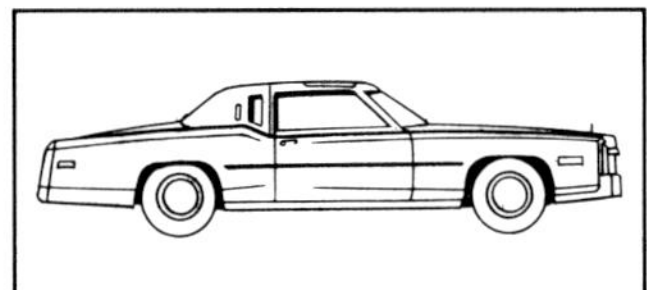

A CAR FOR A CHANGING AMERICA 1977–1992

1977

The Automobile

The 1977 General Motors full-sized cars were downsized and lightened for 1977 — the General's first meaningful response to unstable oil supplies and prices. The results put GM ahead of its American counterparts, and the megabuck risk of redesigning paid off handsomely. The full-sized Cadillac de Villes managed to retain their identities with new, lean, sharp-edged styling and an admirable margin of performance and efficiency. The 472-cid engine was replaced by a 425-cid unit, the first decrease in engine size in post–World War II Cadillac history.

The Calais series was dropped, making the de Ville the entry-level Cadillac by default. Since most effort was spent on the new de Ville, the Eldorado and Seville only received minor face-lifts and subtle mechanical changes. The Eldorado received the 425-cid engine in place of the 500-cid unit, and Seville was fitted with four-wheel disk brakes.

Lincoln introduced its own competitor to the wildly successful Seville with a thinly disguised Mercury Monarch sedan called the Versailles. Continental styling cues alone do not make a Lincoln, and luxury car buyers rejected the Versailles. By 1980 it had vanished quietly; it is best forgotten. Nevertheless, the newly restyled Continental Mark V coupe was a hit, and it readily outsold the handsome Eldorado coupe.

1977 in Miniature

The 1/25-scale Jo-Han Eldorado promotional disappeared in 1977, although it would have been easy enough to modify the 1976 version to make it available.

Jo-Han had not given up making Cadillac models, however. The big news for 1977 was the downsized de Ville, and Jo-Han made 1/25-scale 1977 plastic promotional models of the Coupe de Ville and painted them in Cadillac colors. The chassis and interiors were left unpainted white plastic.

1977

Jo-Han (USA): Coupe de Ville, 1/25, plastic promo; obsolete; less common. **$8 – 20**

1977, 1978, and 1979 Jo-Han plastic promos of Coupe de Villes. Promotional models have white interiors while snap kits (from the same mold) have body-colored interiors.

1978

The Automobile

Since 1977 was a major restyling year, the 1978 models had few differences. Real wire wheels were optional on de Ville and Seville. California-bound Sedan de Villes were equipped with lightweight aluminum hoods to keep the heavily loaded sedans in a lower EPA weight-limit class. The Eldorado Biarritz became a coupe since the convertible was history. An AM/FM/CB radio with tape player was available for the first time to keep passengers entertained.

1978 in Miniature

Jo-Han warmed over its 1977 Cadillac de Ville model dies to produce a 1⁄25-scale promotional model. The promotionals were molded in white plastic, assembled, and painted in Cadillac colors. Eldorado and Seville were completely ignored once again.

1978

Jo-Han (USA) P 2678: Coupe de Ville, 1⁄25, plastic promo; obsolete; less common. Some old stock still available through Ex-El. **$8 – 20**

1979

The Automobile

Cadillac restyled and downsized the Eldorado in 1979. The Seville was scheduled to get its first major reworking in 1980. Overseas, Iran exploded in revolution, and another gas crunch sent motorists scurrying back to small cars once again. It was tough for car companies to predict the ups and downs of the car market after such a rosy 1978, and they were caught unprepared once again. However, when the government mandated odd-even license plate number days for gasoline buyers, Cadillac's fuel-efficient Oldsmobile diesel engine option proved a popular package for the difficult times.

1979 in Miniature

Again, Jo-Han made a 1⁄25-scale promotional and even a snap-kit model of the Coupe de Ville from the same mold. This was to be the final year for any plastic promotional model of a current model year Cadillac. The promotional models were molded in white plastic, assembled, and painted in Cadillac colors, while the snap-together kits came unassembled and molded in red plastic. In a fit of whimsy Jo-Han would sometimes inexplicably include a 1977 or 1978 Coupe de Ville in the snap-kit box rather than the 1979. Perhaps this was one way to eliminate old stock, but for the collector the box was no help in determining contents. Assembled, the snap-kit models cannot be told apart from the

Two color variations of Tomica's die-cast 1979 Eldorado-powered Panther 6

promotionals except for the color of the plastic. This is most confusing to collectors — and rightly so!

Sadly, most modelmakers ignored the new Eldorado and the last year of the rear-drive Seville. What a wasted opportunity. Only plucky cottage-industry TKM Models (USA) offered a 1⁄25-scale 1979 Eldorado in a resin kit. This particular kit could be ordered with opaque windows or with opened windows and a scale interior!

The only other bright spot in a lean miniature Cadillac year was a tiny Japanese 1⁄67-scale die-cast Tomica Pocket Car of the wonderfully wacky Eldorado-powered British Panther 6 exoticar. The real six-wheeled car was probably inspired by the six-wheeled Tyrell Formula One Grand Prix racer of the 1970s, and few of these obscure but sporty Panther two-seaters for the rich were actually built. Its twin-axle steering system would probably have given the boys down at the local alignment shop nightmares anyway. The tiny Tomica Panther was a remarkably well-proportioned replica that came in two-tone blue and silver or two-tone red and silver.

1979

Jo-Han (USA) P 2779: Coupe de Ville, 1⁄25, plastic promo; current; less common. Available through Ex-El. **$8 – 15**

Jo-Han (USA): Coupe de Ville, 1⁄25, plastic kit; red; current; less common. Snap kit taken from promo mold. **$3 – 7**

Tomica Pocket Cars (Japan) F14: Panther 6, 1⁄67, die-cast; blue/silver or red/silver; current; less common. Wonderful exoticar with Eldorado drive train and six wheels. **$5 – 12**

1980

The Automobile

Although the new full-sized de Ville and Fleetwood Broughams were reskins of existing chassis, Cadillacs still looked like proper Cadillacs. Gone was the silky 425-cid V-8, and a new more economical 368-cid V-8 was standard. An optional Oldsmobile 350-cid diesel continued as an optional power plant. Eldorado was largely unchanged, but Seville switched from rear-drive to front-drive and gained a controversial new body shape, the rear of which was reminiscent of a Hooper-bodied Rolls Royce. Eldorado outsold the new downsized Continental Mark VI, and Seville sales left the ugly duckling Ford Granada-based Versailles in the dust. Cadillac sales were still off, but the economy was in recession, so everyone suffered to some degree.

1980 in Miniature

TKM Models commemorated the new reskinned Fleetwood four-door with a 1⁄25-scale resin kit. The TKM Fleetwood could be ordered with opaque windows or with open windows and a scale interior. This was the only 1⁄25-scale version of this body style.

The new bustle-back Seville inspired a small fleet of miniatures. Aurore Models of Switzerland made a low-production 1⁄43-scale resin kit. Not particularly accurate or even attractive, the Seville was not up to Aurore's usual standard; one supposes that the designer never saw a real Seville.

Marcast (USA) toys sold a limited-edition 1⁄20-scale cast-metal 1980 Seville De Elegance reminiscent of the great, collectible, cast-iron Arcade toy cars of the 1930s. In

Marcast's cast-aluminum 1980 Seville, done in the style of classic cast-iron Arcade toys

***Top:** Tomica die-cast 1980 Sevilles (note opening doors). **Middle:** Variations of Mattel Hot Wheels die-cast Sevilles. **Bottom:** Two variations of Yatming die-cast Sevilles and two Tintoy die-casts (odd rear license plate looks like coiled fire hose), which appear to be copies of the Tomica on the top shelf.*

his rural Virginia workshop — where he also created specialized props and full-sized vehicles for the movies — Marcast's Marty Martino designed, cast (both rubber and metal parts), and handpainted less than 125 examples of his mini-Seville. It may not have appealed to all collectors because of its toylike appearance and dizzying $250 original issue price tag, but it was never intended as a high-tech model. This was a rugged toy probably best left for well-heeled junior Cadillac connoisseurs to push around the floor only on their Oriental rugs. In defense of the model's high price and lack of fine detail, one must remember that short-run, handmade collectibles such as these are painstaking, time-consuming enterprises produced by individual hobbyist/builders who do not enjoy help from outside suppliers, costly promotion, and distribution networks already in place. Such products thus become more exciting finds because they are truly folk-art labors of love, albeit at a price.

Mattel Hot Wheels (USA/Hong Kong) issued a 3⅛" die-cast Seville Elegante in silver and purple or metallic gold. Some examples of the gold version came equipped with simulated aftermarket wheel rims shod with "GOODYEAR" white-lettered tires. Proportions were not great, but then these were always intended to be inexpensive toys and not exact scale models.

Tomica Pocket Cars (Japan) currently offers a tiny 1/69-scale Seville that is of fine quality and low price. The standard blister-pack issue is painted a flawless metallic gold, and one can only fault the nonauthentic generic mag wheels. Special versions produced for the Japanese home market and for gift sets were specially two-toned in silver and blue or silver and red to simulate the optional Elegante paint scheme.

Copyrights and patents are vague in the Orient, and Hong Kong-based Tintoys (a misnomer) made what appeared to be a die-cast copy of the Tomica Seville

(Tintoys #WT8307). These copies came in a variety of colors and had black plastic bumpers more suited to a Checker cab! The folks at Tintoys had imagination, for the rear license plate was replaced by what looked like a coil of fire hose. One wonders if a fire chief's version was originally planned!

Yatming (Thailand) also made a die-cast copy of the Tomica Seville. Marginally better finished than the Tintoys copy, the Yatming version sported a custom silkscreened side stripe with "Cadillac" and "Seville Elegante" script. Yatming also equipped its Seville with black plastic bumpers and wild colors. These were inexpensive toys found on the kiddy toy rack at the grocery or drug store.

An unknown maker created a 1/35-scale, chrome-plated, slush-cast, Seville bank that would be right at home on the "executive junque gifts" counter at the airport gift shop. The detail was minimal, and the wheels were cast right to the body so that the bank would not roll off the dresser top. A huge coin slot was cut out of the rear window.

1980

Aurore Models (Switzerland) 15: Seville, 1/43, resin kit, unpainted; obsolete; very rare. Limited production. **$20 – 40**

Martino (USA): Seville toy, 1/20, cast aluminum; blue/gray; obsolete; rarest. **$125 – 300**

Mattel Hot Wheels (USA/Hong Kong) 1698: Seville Elegante, 3⅛", die-cast; silver/purple or gold; obsolete; less common. Gold version comes with standard hot wheel or Goodyear RWL. **$1 – 3**

Tintoys (Hong Kong) WT8307: Seville, 1/69, die-cast; current; common. Copy of Tomica F45; odd coiled fire hose at rear license plate. **$.50 – 1**

Tomica Pocket Cars (Japan) F45: Seville, 1/69, die-cast; gold, red/silver, or blue/silver; current; less common. Two-tone version originally from gift set. **$1 – 5**

Unknown: Seville, 1/35, slush-cast metal; chrome or silver plated; obsolete; rare. One-piece bank with coin slot in rear window. **$15 – 30**

Yatming (Thailand) 1026: Seville, 1/69, die-cast; metallic paint and graphics; current; common. Copy of Tomica F45; black bumpers; "Seville Elegante" trim. **$.50 – 2**

1981–1986

The Automobile

The biggest news for 1981 Cadillacs was the adoption of the variable displacement V-8-6-4 engine. Theoretically, this landmark engineering achievement would allow the Cadillac V-8 to operate as a V-8, a V-6, or a V-4 — depending upon power needs. A microprocessor monitored performance data and automatically switched modes for best economy and drivability. It was a great idea on paper, but reliability problems plagued the V-8-6-4, and it was only used on limousines after the 1981 model year, and it disappeared entirely soon after.

The Oldsmobile diesel engine was again an option for 1981, but it was also plagued by reliability problems. A third option was a Buick-built 252-cid V-6 engine! For a company whose history was tied so closely with the development of the V-8 engine, this seemed like a step backwards, and certainly performance of the big Cadillacs suffered as a result. Cadillac was not the only one having trouble selling luxury cars. Lincoln's uninspired line also caused its sales to flag. The floundering Chrysler Corporation fielded a reskinned Cordoba as an Imperial at a stiff sticker price of over $18,000! These were grim times for America's prestige makes, and the public increasingly looked to foreign makes to meet their auto needs.

After all of the problems with 1981 Cadillac engine offerings, the 1982 Eldorado, Fleetwood, de Ville, and Seville were all equipped with the new aluminum 249-cid V-8 engine, the smallest American production V-8. Performance was smooth and dependable — but leisurely at best. Mercifully, the troublesome diesel was dropped from the Seville's standard equipment roster.

Another 1982 addition to the Cadillac line was the Cimarron, the first four-cylinder Caddy since 1905! Although it handled well and was an automobile assembled with close attention to detail, it was underpowered and easily mistaken for less expensive J-body variants from other GM divisions. This identity crisis would eventually prove to be its undoing.

The 1983 Cadillac line saw no major styling changes. New grilles, interiors, and trim packages freshened the line. The Buick-built V-6 disappeared from full-sized Cadillac option lists, and the Cimarron picked up a new 2.0-liter four-cylinder with throttle-body fuel injection to counter criticism about lack of power.

The 1984 Cadillacs were essentially carryovers from 1983. The biggest news was the return of the Eldorado Biarritz convertible.

Resin kits from TKM. ***Top:*** *1985 Fleetwood.* ***Bottom:*** *1986 Seville (raw resin kit before finishing or painting).*

Actually, Cadillac was still out of the convertible-building business, for the production of the new Eldorado ragtop was farmed out to ASC Corporation, the same company that had produced the natty Buick Riviera convertible in 1983. Partially finished Eldorados were shipped to ASC to be chopped and modified to GM specification.

Although originally scheduled for introduction at the end of 1983, the new generation of front-drive Fleetwoods and de Villes did not debut until 1985 because of transmission development problems.

Cadillac trod a dangerous path, for it wanted both to retain its traditional buyers and attract younger affluent buyers away from attractive foreign luxury makes. The silky 4.1-liter V-8 engine was the standard engine for all models (except Cimarron) and had the distinction of being the world's only transverse-mounted V-8 front driver when used in the new C-body Fleetwoods and de Villes. A 4.3-liter V-6 diesel engine was a no-cost option.

The 1985 Cimarron gained sales momentum and was offered for the first time with a zippy 2.8-liter V-6 that increased Cimarron's horsepower by a whopping 46 percent! Critics of Cimarron's lackluster acceleration were silenced, and Cimarron was at last a proper yuppie sporting sedan.

The 1986 Eldorado and Seville were completely restyled. The new shortened Eldorado could not be modified into a convertible, and so the Eldorado convertible disappeared once again. The Seville shared its mechanical underpinnings with Eldorado, and (unfortunately) much of its new look, too. Critics panned the new styling as too much like that used on less expensive GM products, despite the fact that the new Seville and Eldorado were simply better cars than the ones they superseded. Optional stiffer "touring" suspensions continued to be offered. These specially equipped cars were distinguished by less gingerbread trim and more subdued colors. Enthusiast magazines still whined about the lack of tire-burning horsepower, but all acknowledged that Cadillac had produced some fine-handling automobiles.

The rear-drive Fleetwood Brougham that could be traced all the way back to 1977 was scheduled to be discontinued in 1985, but the lukewarm public reaction to the new front-drive Fleetwood, de Ville, Eldorado, and Seville gave Cadillac second thoughts. Rather than alienating more traditional Cadillac buyers, the Fleetwood Brougham sedan was given a new lease on life and a Chevrolet-built 5.0-liter V-8 engine.

1981–1986 in Miniature

Cadillac's hard times in the 1980s were reflected in miniature also. No major toy or model companies seemed interested in modeling Cadillacs of that decade. Only cottage-industry TKM Models offered a 1/25-scale resin kit of the 1985 front-drive Sedan de Ville and the 1986 Seville. The Seville could be ordered with opaque windows or open windows with interior. Perhaps the model- and toymakers noted the less-than-enthusiastic public reactions to the new Cadillacs and feared that their miniature versions might be doomed to the same fate. Then again, maybe they were too busy modeling the Mercedes, Porsches, Ferraris, Lamborghinis, Camaros, and Firebirds that had captured young America's hearts and become the icons of pop culture that had displaced Cadillac. It is interesting to note that many of the miniatures of the most outrageous Cadillacs of the 1940s and 1950s were made and sold in the 1980s, thus indicating a nostalgia for what the Cadillac once represented to the American dream.

1986

TKM (USA): Fleetwood, 1/25, resin kit, unpainted; obsolete; less common. **$20 – 35**

TKM (USA): Seville, 1/25, resin kit, unpainted; obsolete; less common. **$20 – 35**

1987–1990

The Automobile

The Mercedes SL-fighting Allante was launched with a flourish in 1987 to mark Cadillac's re-entry into the ultra-luxury car market. Pininfarina designed and manufactured the bodies in Turin, Italy, and shipped them, fifty-six at a time, in special air-cargo modules on Alitalia or Lufthansa Boeing 747 airfreighters to final assembly in Detroit over three thousand miles away. There, specially trained Allante workers added specially tweaked Eldorado running gear, making the Allante "air bridge" the longest assembly line in the world.

The Cimarron was given suspension refinements and more horsepower by modifications to the V-6 engine. It was also equipped with a streamlined composite headlight system that gave front styling more Cadillac corporate identity. Even though the Cimarron had been refined into a fine compact road machine, its disappointing sales would kill it in another year. One cannot help but wonder if a Cimarron convertible based upon the same body as the successful J-body Chevy Cavalier and Pontiac Sunbird ragtops would have given Cimarron added appeal and sales. Another missed opportunity.

De Ville and Fleetwood front-drivers were stretched a subtle one-and-a-half inches with new fender/bumper-end caps and a new grille with composite headlights. The 60 Special, with its own longer wheelbase, returned to the line. Interestingly, the Fleetwood 75 limousine was also built on a stretched front-drive platform.

Seville and Eldorado were still fresh designs from the previous model year, but customer resistance necessitated a crash restyling for the Eldorado for 1988 to return some of the traditional Cadillac flavor to an otherwise modern but dull design.

A new burst of creativity at Cadillac styling produced the striking Voyage sedan and Solitaire coupe concept cars that toured show circuits respectively in 1989 and 1990, wowing audiences and forecasting exciting new cars to come.

Cadillac also received the coveted Malcolm Baldridge Award for Excellence in 1990, a major coup for new leadership at GM after president Roger Smith's retirement. The lessons of the last decade were not lost on top management, and the 1990s promised more autonomy for each of the General's divisions in product identity and design.

1987–1990 in Miniature

Toymakers liked the Allante from the start. Matchbox (Macau) makes a nice 1/60-scale die-cast Allante roadster in silver, Mary Kay pink, and black (with unattractive "laser" wheels and tacky contrasting silkscreened graphics). Packed on a bubble card and still available wherever popular Matchbox toys are sold, this tiny Allante is inexpensive and fun, and it may be the new dream car of young Cadillac fans.

Majorette (France) also models the Allante in close to 1/60 scale, but its die-cast version does not come off as well as the Matchbox version. In fact, the front of the Majorette Allante looks more like the front of a Pontiac Phoenix X-car.

TKM Models made a 1/25-scale resin kit of the Allante that sported a full interior. This was a needed model to fill out a 1/25-scale Cadillac collection, and it took a bold cottage-industry modelmaker to realize it.

An unknown manufacturer made a 1/43-scale pewter Allante that was sold by some Cadillac dealers at their parts counters. Some of these pewter two-seaters even came with lucite bases decorated with the elegant Allante script. Paint, windows, and detailing would make this a much nicer model.

A 1991 release of great interest is a die-cast 1/43-scale Maloney 1990 Cadillac stretch limousine by Kim's Classics of England. Complete with photo-etched details and glossy paintwork, this handmade model is museum quality. Since the model comes packed in a Western Models box, one may assume that Kim's farmed out actual production to Western's experienced craftsmen. The results show a high standard of finish.

For those who do not want to spend $250 on the lovely Kim's Classic limo, Majorette of France currently makes a very popular 1/58-scale die-cast 1987 Cadillac "stretch" limousine with opening doors, a sliding passenger sunroof, and even a boomerang-style television antenna on the rear deck! The initial black-painted release was followed by metallic gray and then white versions. This is a popular toy/model and one of the few limousine models made. The really glaring flaw on the Majorette

1987 Allantes. ***Left to right:*** *Matchbox first issue, very pink Matchbox die-cast, "World Class" Series (with mirrored windows and extra detailing) and "Laser Wheel" versions of Matchbox die-casts, and Majorette die-cast.* ***Behind them:*** *Alitalia Boeing 747 air cargo freighter, Schuco metal, from the "air bridge" portion of the Allante trans-Atlantic assembly line.*

The prestige of the Cadillac automobile and the popularity of Cadillac miniatures have led to all sorts of uses of models. Here the Matchbox 1987 Allante has been encased in the bottom of a lucite old-fashioned glass as a promotional item.

model is the choice of wheels; the whizzwheels it uses would look better on a truck or a Jeep. However, for the low price of less than three dollars, this is a minor gripe.

Galoob Micromachines (USA) is the only company to model the futuristic 1989 Voyage show car in a 1¼" toy with the tiny free-spinning wheels that make such pocket racers so popular with kids.

Nobody makes a model of the beautifully stark Solitaire concept car yet.

Mattel Hot Wheels (Malaysia) offers a customized 3¼" stretch limousine based on the 1990 front-drive Fleetwood 75 limousine and calls it the "Limozeen." The grillework seems more typical of a Lincoln or even the short-lived Zimmer, but the body shape and rear fender caps are all

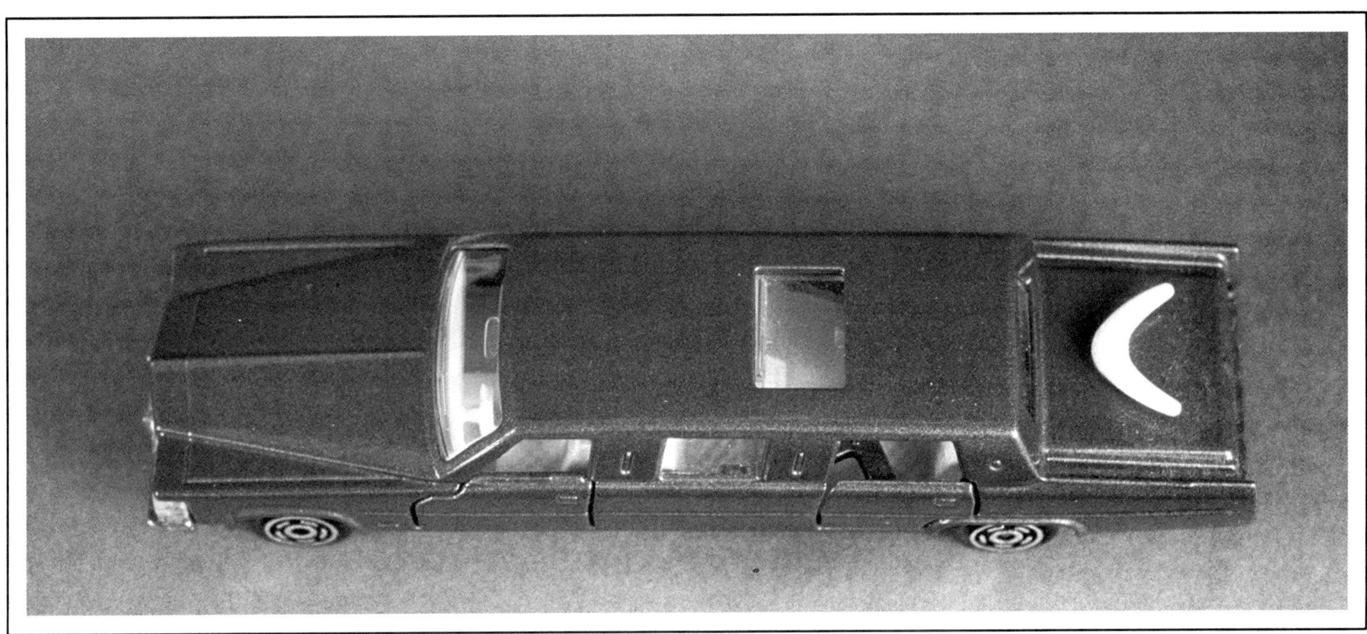

Check out the sliding sunroof and trunk-mounted TV antenna on this die-cast Majorette stretch limo.

The museum quality of the Kim's Classics miniature of this 1990 limousine is evident in the accuracy of every detail.

1987 Allante, as resin kit from TKM

***On left:** 1950 die-cast sedan (with key-wind motor) from Solido and 1990 custom "Limozeen" by Mattel Hot Wheels.*
***Far right:** 1989 "Voyage" show car from Galoob Micromachines.*

Cadillac. The first version is white with trendy California-style silkscreened graphics that read "VJ Classic Limo Service".

Unfortunately, the Eldorado, Seville, and Cimarron have not been modeled in scale. It is to be hoped that modelmakers will realize this oversight.

1987

Majorette (France) 339: stretch limousine, 1⁄58, die-cast; black, white, or metallic gray/brown; current; common. Sliding sunroof, trunk-mounted TV antenna. **$1 – 3**

Matchbox (GB): Allante, 1⁄60, die-cast; silver or pink; black version with "laser" disk wheels also available; current; common. "World Class" series has mirrored windows. **$.50 – 2**

TKM (USA): Allante, 1⁄25, resin kit, unpainted; obsolete; common. **$20 – 35**

Unknown: Allante, 1⁄43, pewter promo; current; less common. Available through Cadillac dealers. **$20 – 55**

1989

Galoob (China): Voyage show car, 1¼", plastic; black; current; common. Micromachine. Cartoonish interpretation. **$.25 – 1**

Paint and windows have been added to this pewter promo of the 1987 Allante (manufacturer unknown).

1990

Kim's Classic (GB): Maloney stretch limousine, 1⁄43, die-cast; black, blue, white, or metallic red; current; less common. Handbuilt, museum quality, expensive. **$125 – 250**

Mattel Hot Wheels (Malaysia) 112: limousine, 3¼", die-cast; white; current; common. "Limozeen" TM. **$.50 – 1.50**

1991–1992

The Automobile

With Robert Stemple at GM's helm, big changes began to take place in all GM divisions, and Cadillac once again asserted itself as a styling and technology leader of GM's new 1990s strategy. In the fall of 1991, Cadillac released their striking new 1992 Eldorado and Seville models. Available with optional "Touring" suspension packages, the new Cadillac offerings proved that American technology and styling could once again produce beautiful high-performance cars.

The 1992 Allante was the first to receive the all-new and powerful 300-horsepower Cadillac-designed four-cam "North Star" engine that is destined to find its way into other models of the Cadillac line, restoring the performance image that languished in the 1980s. In addition, the North Star–powered Allante was chosen to pace the Indianapolis 500 in 1992, making it the sixth Cadillac product to earn this coveted honor since 1927!

1991–1992 in Miniature

At this writing, no one has yet offered models of the sleek new Eldorado or Seville. Since the lovely Pinanfarina-designed Allante has not changed cosmetically since its 1987 introduction, the descriptions of the Matchbox and Majorette models would also apply here. Let's hope that a model company will give Allante its due and duplicate the handsome red 1992 Indy pace car in scale, too.

Conclusion

Cadillac's reputation for excellence is automotive legend. The popularity of Cadillac models and toys has reflected the public's acceptance of America's own dream machine as a symbol of quality and success for over three-quarters of the century. Those who love great automobiles appreciate the traditions of style, fine engineering, innovation, and magic in the Cadillac name.

INDEX OF MINIATURES BY MANUFACTURER

The page numbers refer to the formal listing of the miniature

About the Author

As the son of a professional automotive engineer, Jeff Gurski grew up with a love of fine automobiles. For the past twenty years he has collected real cars and has assembled an exceptional miniature automobile collection that focuses on American cars, particularly Cadillac. He is known for his special expertise and insight into this prestigious GM marque, and over the years he has authored a popular series of articles for the Cadillac Club International magazine, *Cadillac Connoisseur,* and for the journal of the Capital Miniature Auto Collectors' Club. His automotive interests are many, though, for he is also a member of the Tucker Automobile Club of America and the National and Washington, D.C. Area Mazda Miata Clubs.

A native of northern Virginia and a graduate of the University of Virginia, he is a Northern Virginia Writing Project Fellow and currently teaches writing in Chantilly, Virginia.

Jeff Gurski with a source of pride — the 1980 Coupe de Ville, once his father's, that he is restoring.